Earthly Delights

Earthly Delights

Tubs of Tomatoes and Buckets of Beans

JACK KRAMER

FULCRUM PUBLISHING
GOLDEN, COLORADO

Book design by Alyssa Pumphrey
Cover illustration by Michael Valdez

Some of the plants referred to in this book or appearing in nature may be poisonous. Any person, particularly a novice gardener, should exercise care in handling or ingesting plants. The publisher and the author accept no responsibility for any damage or injury resulting from the use or ingesting of, or contact with any plant discussed in this book.

Library of Congress Cataloging-in-Publication Data

Kramer, Jack
        Earthly delights : tubs of tomatoes and buckets of beans / Jack Kramer.
                p.   cm.
        Includes index.
        ISBN 1-55591-264-8 (pbk.)
                1. Vegetable gardening. 2. Container gardening. I. Title.
        SB324.4.K73   1997
        635'.048—dc21   96-48839
                                                                        CIP

Printed in the United States of America
0 9 8 7 6 5 4 3 2 1

Fulcrum Publishing
350 Indiana Street, Suite 350
Golden, Colorado 80401-5093
(800) 992-2908 • (303) 277-1623

Contents

Contents

Author's Note

Today, dozens of vegetable seed mail-order suppliers exist throughout the country. There are also local nurseries that carry prepack vegetables, so literally hundreds of different varieties are available. It would be impossible for me to list every good variety. Therefore I have listed a limited number of choices.

Buy your seeds and prepacks to suit your own weather conditions and personal preferences, and consult the many mail order catalogs advertised in garden magazines and at the back of this book.

No matter which variety you grow, how to grow them is the most important aspect of having a good harvest. I have concentrated on culture and landscaping with vegetables and growing them mainly in container situations. Vegetables are surely earthly delights.

This book contains a special section (see chapter 11) on various ethnic vegetables. My recommendations are general, for more specific data check cookbooks in your library.

Preface

You do not need a vast outdoor garden or acres of land to grow fine vegetables and herbs, strawberries, or even tropicals such as avocados and bananas. There is a veritable indoor Eden available to you when you grow plants in containers.

In planters or boxes, pots or garbage cans—you name it—you can grow a fine crop of edibles. Obviously you can buy various containers, but you can also make your own containers from wood.

Container gardening is a well-documented way of growing plants easily because you select the appropriate soil, and you can move plants to patio or porch or have them indoors as well. You can grow climbing vegetables, such as cucumbers and green peppers, on trellises in pots if space is limited. There is a whole new world of earthly delights awaiting you.

And do not forget the dwarf vegetables now available such as small Japanese eggplant, cucumbers, peppers, and other fine produce. Asian vegetables and Mexican produce can be cultivated too. The selection of edibles is large if you know what plants to grow and how to grow them. Welcome to nature's cupboard—the world of earthly delights—as we create fresh, wonderful vegetables with ease and enjoyment and throw in a few recipes as well to delight the palate. Bon appétit!

CHAPTER 1

The Advantages of Container Gardening

Gardening in containers is certainly not new. The Hanging Gardens of Babylon, the Adonis Gardens in Greece, the Domitian Palace in Rome, the Moorish gardens in Spain—these ancient places were decorated with plants growing in beautifully decorated pots. Oranges in tubs and fancy urns brimming with flowered plants abounded throughout Europe. Ancient civilizations knew what modern gardeners have rediscovered, that gardening in containers affords numerous pluses, including portability, less damage from insects, and beauty. Vegetables are perfect plants for container growing because they do well in the confined space of a planter or pot rather than being subjected to bacteria and other harmful organisms they would encounter if growing in the ground.

PORTABILITY AND BEAUTY

The right containers for your vegetables—containers that are not too heavy or too large—are easy to move around when you want and where you want, saving you backbreaking labor. Commercially made boxes and planters have the bonus of coming with dollies, which really make moving easy. Containers on the deck, patio, porch, balcony, or terrace add a touch of distinction and a dollop of enjoyable food.

Deck Garden

Michael Valdez

Decorative pots, those called jardinieres, especially add beautiful accents of color to a patio or terrace. They are easy to move around and arrange in a pleasant design. For the deck or backyard garden, planters and boxes impart a handsome look, particularly when they are custom-made to fit specific areas. Chapter 4 discusses how to make these containers; for now, just remember that you should not use treated wood, which contains chemical preservatives that are toxic to vegetables and other plants. Use standard cedar or Douglas fir, both of which will last a long time. Boxes and planters can also be arranged in creative arrangements, such as stacked rows, which enable you to tend plants easily without stooping or bending.

No matter where your vegetable garden is located, whether on a deck, balcony, patio, terrace, or in the city backyard, containers are the answer. Both versatile and attractive, pots, boxes, and planters will all help you enjoy your earthly harvest.

INDOORS OR OUTDOORS

Today, because of hybridization and better breeding, many vegetables are quite suitable for growing indoors as well as outside. Indoors, the answer again is obviously containers, from terra cotta pots to jardinieres to hanging baskets. The dwarf or midget varieties of tomatoes, green peppers, beets, cucumbers, peas, and carrots are all ideal for the indoor garden, allowing you the luxury of plucking your own food crops while preparing a dish of vegetables for your nightly meal. You can raise your bounty in the kitchen, in a greenhouse, or in a garden room, and indoors you can even dry, can, or freeze the

Deck Garden Plants

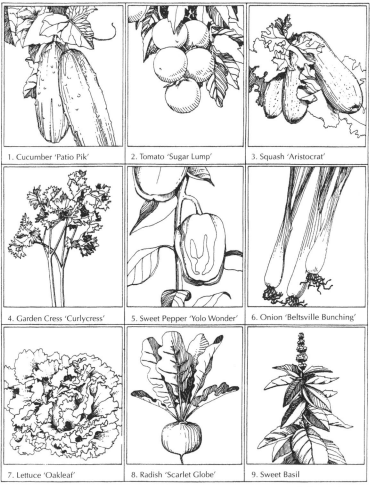

1. Cucumber 'Patio Pik'   2. Tomato 'Sugar Lump'   3. Squash 'Aristocrat'

4. Garden Cress 'Curlycress'   5. Sweet Pepper 'Yolo Wonder'   6. Onion 'Beltsville Bunching'

7. Lettuce 'Oakleaf'   8. Radish 'Scarlet Globe'   9. Sweet Basil

Robert Johnson

food for future meals (see methods for storing vegetables in chapter 7). If you do not have the inclination to or the conditions for raising vegetables outside, consider the delights of growing crops inside. Not only will the vegetables be good eating, but while they are growing in their containers they will be pretty houseplants as well.

THWARTING INSECTS AND ANIMALS

Aphids, leaf borers, worms, beetles, gophers, moles, slugs, and snails will all raid your outdoor vegetable garden that is growing in the ground. With no fondness I recall the gophers in my California vegetable garden: They ate as much of the produce as I did!

Getting rid of insects and animal pests is not easy when the plants are in the ground, but when growing in containers, vegetables are able to fight off the few invaders that attack. Most pests just will not climb up the containers to get to the vegetables. It is much easier for pests to go elsewhere for their food.

TASTE AND HEALTH

Of course, growing your own vegetables saves money, but more important are the benefits of good taste and health. You do not have to wait for certain vegetables to be in season at your local supermarket; you can just grow them yourself for when you want them, and not when commercial growers dictate they should be available. And the taste of freshly picked homegrown vegetables is incomparable to that of the vegetables shipped long distances in refrigerated trucks from California to Florida or Florida to California, for example. Most commercial vegetables are picked while they are still green, so you do not get the full rich taste from the crops.

We all know how healthful vegetables are, but homegrown ones are even more healthful than commercially grown ones because no preservatives or insecticides have been used on them. Vitamins are also lost during transportation of commercial vegetables but not in crops picked fresh at the moment you want them.

THE BIG PLUS

The big asset from growing your own vegetables is the ultimate satisfaction you get from knowing that you grew it yourself. Whether you grow the exotic vegetables that are hard to find, such as escarole or bok choy, or raise the old tried-and-true standards, you will have the thrill of raising your own "offshoots." You will have a tremendous sense of accomplishment and a joy of working with nature. Raise your own delicious food crops, and enjoy yourself in the process.

CHAPTER 2

Planning the Vegetable Garden

Over the years, scientists and growers have developed superb hybrid vegetables that will do well in your container garden. Your selection depends first on the geographical area you live in (climate), because vegetables are cool- or warm-season. For example, tomatoes, eggplant, squash, and cucumbers must be planted in warm weather (and soil), to grow on into summer; beets, spinach, lettuce, and cauliflower should be planted in midsummer or very early spring so they can mature before hot weather sets in. Other factors can affect what to grow, including the amount of space and time that you can devote to vegetables, personal taste, and whether you want to use seeds or prestarts.

Begin your vegetable garden with the more popular, easy plants such as lettuce, beets, carrots, tomatoes, and beans (corn needs too much space, and potatoes are not easy to grow). The following year, after you have some experience, you can focus on the more exotic vegetables. Do not try to grow everything at once. Use your available space wisely: Plant prestarts (discussed later) at the recommended distances, and use walls, trellises, or poles for the climbers such as cucumbers and squash. A 10 x 20 foot garden can accommodate carrots, radishes, tomatoes, cucumbers, eggplant, and squash, more than enough food to keep you going. By August or September, the food crops are usually spent, but you can revitalize the same plot with winter crops such as peppers and pole beans.

LOCATION OF PLANTS

Vegetables need light and sun. A balcony, patio or terrace, doorway, backyard, rooftop, or deck are all ideal places for your vegetables in containers if the areas receive plenty of light.

Kitchen Garden

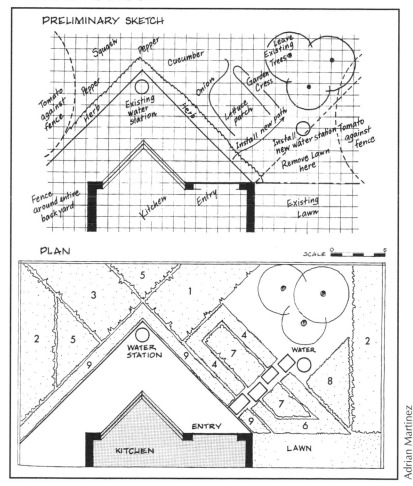

Adrian Martinez

1. Cucumber 'Patio Pik'
2. Tomato 'Sugar Lump'
3. Squash 'Aristocrat'
4. Garden Cress 'Curlycress'
5. Sweet Pepper 'Yolo Wonder'
6. Onion 'Beltsville Bunching'
7. Lettuce 'Oakleaf'
8. Radish 'Scarlet Globe'
9. Sweet Basil

7

Balconies

Balconies in high-rise buildings are perfect for growing vegetables on trellises. Squash and cucumbers will thrive here; a few pots of herbs at floor level will balance the garden. Avoid too many plants or the balcony will become a jungle.

Do not forget safety considerations. A container filled with soil can seriously injure someone below if it falls off a ledge. Keep all containers at floor level, including wooden planters and boxes. All containers should be well anchored too because balconies are very windy under certain conditions. Wind also dries out plants, so have a watering can handy. Finally, be sure to shield plants with screens from the intense noon sun.

Patios and Terraces

Today the patio or terrace serves as an extra room for entertaining, relaxation, and a garden room for both plants and vegetables. Wood planters and boxes are appropriate on the patio or terrace, but some additional decoration is needed, such as that jardinieres or glazed pots provide. (Chapter 4 discusses the specifics of containers; here we consider how to arrange the decorative pots that will enliven your patio or terrace.) You also have to consider what type of flooring you will use for your patio or terrace.

Containers arranged in a triangular design rather than in rigid rows have a much more dynamic look and feel. But if this fluid form does not suit your taste, try grouping the containers in just one area, perhaps a corner—use three or five pots in each selected location. Not only is this a commanding look, but watering and tending the vegetables will be easier because the plants are in one spot rather than scattered around the patio or terrace.

No matter how you group your containers, be sure you have ample room for garden furniture and walking space. The flooring should be planned too: Consider how the floor material will weather, if it is comfortable to walk on, and how it looks. Brick is handsome but gets slippery and grimy when wet. Gravel is effective and can be replaced as necessary. Slate and fir bark are other very suitable materials. (Avoid ground fir bark because it invariably looks messy.)

Doorways

Midget cucumbers, tiny tomatoes, and an assortment of herbs will do well and look attractive in a doorway garden. Remember to select small plants so they do not become overbearing. And be sure to consider traffic: Too many containers will get in people's way, but a few containers on one side will be fine.

City Backyards

In a small backyard, the ornamental garden of trees and shrubs may be out of scale with the house or high-rise building. A vegetable garden, grown in a planter bed, will look wonderful in this location. If the light is limited, grow carrots, beets, spinach, and lettuce; with sufficient sun, any vegetable crop will grow well. The backyard of a high-rise is also a great spot for community vegetable growing.

The advantage of a planter bed, rather than growing directly in the soil of the backyard, is that you supply the correct type of soil; you do not have to work with the old soil in the ground or try to revitalize it. Cool- or warm-season vegetables work well here, depending on your climate. You can start seeds right in the outdoor bed if weather permits, begin vegetables indoors, or move them to the planter bed when frost is over. Just be sure to regularly water and feed the plants.

The Backyard Container Garden

The backyard container garden lets you grow vegetables in suitable containers and provides you with a way to tend the food crops easily. Wood planters and boxes work best if the backyard garden will be extensive. The planters and boxes look great in the backyard and are inexpensive to make (see chapter 4) in almost any size you want. In fact, one handy size is waist-high; with this height you can avoid stooping and bending, which is important if you have back problems. Build the container waist-high, or insert wood blocks under a shorter one to elevate it to the desired height.

Be sure the vegetable containers are conveniently located near water outlets, and provide ample drainage. Also install enough drainage canals for water to run off your property—you do not want standing water after a rain.

Have wide paths—at least 40 inches—around the containers so you can get to the plants. A gravel walk is inexpensive to install, comfortable to walk on, and almost maintenance-free. White gravel is particularly attractive and lasts 2 to 3 years before needing replacement.

Grow garden plants with your vegetables because the mix looks attractive. Use all existing trees and shrubs; your vegetable garden will fit in with your established plants. The vegetables you decide to grow can be accommodated easily in planters and boxes of various shapes and sizes. Place the containers so they are in balance with the garden—one planter on one side and one on the other side looks dull and unbalanced. Follow some of the plans detailed in this book. In addition, besides balance, consider unity and proportion, two other vital aspects of landscaping in any situation. Just be sure you do not have a helter-skelter look to your garden.

10

Fencing is important in the backyard container garden because it completes the picture, framing the landscape as a whole. Wood fencing is the best; wire fencing is also suitable. Before installing the fencing, check with neighbors to see if they approve and/or want to contribute to the project in return for some of the bounty. Abide by local codes: In most areas, 6 feet is the maximum height allowed.

If you do not like the basic rectangular garden, consider a garden in the round, using round tubs and large clay pots within the rectangular plan.

Deck Gardens

So many of us live outdoors on the deck or porch when weather permits that a vegetable garden in these areas is ideal, providing visual interest and enjoyable food. Use planters on the deck, as natural barriers at the perimeter of the deck, and insert trellises into the boxes for climbing beans or cucumbers. Be sure there is sufficient walking and maneuvering room for people and pets.

Plants on decks or porches are often subjected to intense sun and wind, so provide shading with an awning or some shrubs or small trees. Vegetables like sun, but intense sun and wind can cause problems.

It is easy to water plants on a deck (the hose usually is nearby), and when mixed in or balancing containers of flowers and shrubs, vegetables will add a handsome effect.

Porch Trellis

front elevation

Michael Valdez

11

PRESTARTS

Prestarts (prepacks) are seedlings sold six or eight to a plastic package. The seedlings are grown in the plastic containers until they are ready to be transplanted into larger containers.

The advantage of prepacks is that you avoid the time and care involved with nurturing seeds. Prepacks cost more than seeds, but you have plants already growing, saving you time.

Nurseries and home stores with nursery sections are the best places for buying prestarts. Note that some vegetables, such as carrots and radishes, must be started from seed, but tomatoes, midget green peppers, eggplants, and many other vegetables are available as prestarts. Care of seedlings is the same as for seeds (see the following section.)

SEEDS

You can begin seeds indoors or outdoors; when ready, the plants grown indoors can be transferred to the outdoor location or kept inside. To grow the seeds indoors, you need the right location, the proper containers, a good growing medium, and the right environmental conditions, such as light and temperature.

Sowing Seed

1. Fill with sterile growing medium and moisten.

2. Sow seeds according to direction on packet. Cover seeds lightly with soil and mist.

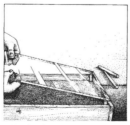

3. Cut dowels to lengths of one-half inch from top of flat; insert dowels in corners on both sides of flat. Top with glass panel or plastic covering to ensure humidity.

4. Remove seedlings for transplanting.

Robert Johnson

GROWING AREAS

Grow seeds in a basement, kitchen, or bathroom that has sufficient space, about 5 to 6 feet wide and 2 to 3 feet long. A secluded area does not interfere with your everyday living, and it is less messy for watering. Keep the temperature constant (about 78° Fahrenheit); if necessary, use electric heating cables, sold at hardware stores, to supply a constant temperature. The cables attach to the bottom of a container or go directly inside it. A cable-and-box container, sold at plant stores, has a built-in device to stabilize temperatures.

Transplanting Seedlings to Pots

13

1. When seedlings are about two inches high and have separate leaves, remove them for transplanting.

2. Take as much of the root ball as possible and place seedlings in small pots.

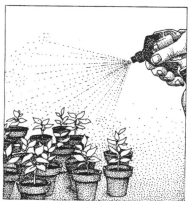

3. Keep the seedlings moist with a fine-mist spray.

4. After a few weeks, transplant to larger pot and place in permanent position at a window, or outdoors if for the garden.

Robert Johnson

Be sure some natural (but not direct) light enters the growing area. (To grow seeds under artificial light, use a closet or dark nook.) Cover the containers with glass or plastic food wrap to ensure adequate humidity, but avoid too much humidity. If lots of condensation appears on the covering, remove the material for a few hours each day. Finally, have a water tap nearby, and keep seed beds waist-high so it is easy to tend to them.

There are a host of containers perfect for seeds. Azalea clay pots are inexpensive and shallow enough for seeds. Wooden flats are 3 to 4 inches high, 16 inches wide, and 20 inches long, with bottom slats $1/2$ inch apart. Nurseries sometimes give away flats.

Any plastic tray is fine for seeds, and the aluminum trays that frozen dinner rolls come in are ideal if you punch drainage holes in the bottom. Milk cartons sliced in half with punched holes in the bottom serve as ideal seed containers, as do coffee cans with punched holes in the bottom.

14

Peat pellets and Kys cubes both work the same way: Embed seeds in the pellets or cubes, water the material (it expands when wet), and set the pellets or cubes directly into a container for permanent growing. With this method you can avoid subjecting seeds to the shock of transplanting.

Growing Medium

Use a sterile medium, or the fungus "damping-off" may attack seeds. Milled sphagnum, vermiculite (expanded mica), perlite (volcanic ash), peat moss and sand, and a mixture of equal parts of vermiculite, sphagnum, and perlite are the five recommended mediums (packaged soils are too heavy for seeds).

Milled sphagnum must be kept evenly moist. Vermiculite retains moisture for a long time. Perlite floats by itself and disturbs the seed bed, so mix it with sterile soil; it retains moisture well.

Moisten a growing medium a few hours beforehand (it is messy otherwise). Constantly keep the medium moist but not soggy while seeds are growing; this is the most important part of sowing seeds.

Planting

Fill the container to within ¹/₄ inch of its top with the pre-moistened growing medium. Scatter seeds on the medium and then press small seeds or embed large seeds into the medium. Water the seeds with a watering can or water from the bottom by soaking the containers in a sink of water. To prevent overwatering, set four sticks in each end of the container and make a tent of clear plastic. The plastic should not touch the medium. Punch some small holes for ventilation in the plastic. When leaves develop, remove the plastic. Remember, the growing medium should be kept evenly moist.

While the seeds are growing, keep them in a sunny or dark spot, at about 78° Fahrenheit, as mentioned earlier. When the plants are a few inches high, thin them out to give weaker plants room to grow. After this thinning, move the vegetable seedlings to a new container, or separately plant each seedling in a permanent container (a second potting encourages much better plants). Tomatoes and cucumbers need large containers (10 to 14 inches in diameter). The next chapter will give you the basics about what kinds of soil to use for transplanting; chapter 4 covers the specific types of containers for your vegetables.

15

Vegetables Indoors

Yes, vegetable gardens can thrive indoors, but some vegetable plants are not overly attractive, so you should restrict the garden to places suitable for food: kitchens, bathrooms, and sunrooms. The following is a discussion of these areas with advice for setting up the veggies in each area. The living room and dining room are also covered, and though I do not care for the appearance of vegetable plants in these areas, you may, so these areas are also discussed.

Kitchens

Kitchens, with their natural humidity from cooking foods, are ideal locations for vegetables. As a bonus, you can pick the leaves of certain vegetables and herbs while you are actually preparing dishes.

Shelves and window setups are the best ways to grow a kitchen vegetable garden. And even areas under shelves will hold, say, small containers of lettuce (use fluorescent lights for these dim places). In windows, you can set up commercially made window-trays that fit most standard windows, make your own glass or wood shelves, or buy the three-tiered units that come knocked down, ready for you to assemble.

Interior Window Garden

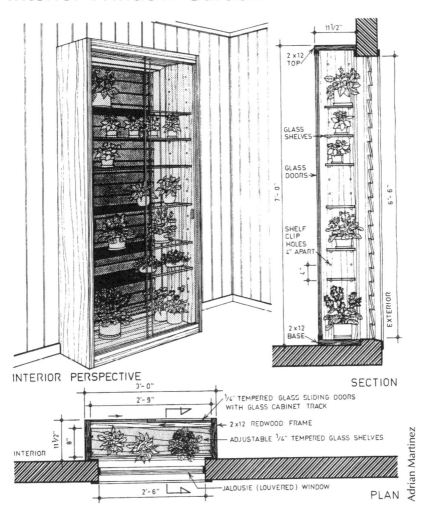

16

INTERIOR PERSPECTIVE

SECTION

PLAN

Adrian Martinez

To install glass shelves, buy $^3/_{16}$-inch-thick-glass with ground (smooth) edges, ready-cut to your specified size, at a glass store. At each end of the window, install 1 x 1 inch wooden strips, to hold each shelf. The shelves sit on top of the strips; the weight of the plants holds the shelves in place. This arrangement will work for double-hung or sliding windows but not hinge-mounted, inside-opening ones.

All your plants on shelves in a window present a uniform picture. To make the vegetable garden especially attractive, use the same type of container for all the plants for visual harmony. White terra cotta pots look particularly nice in the kitchen.

An indoor window box is also useful in the kitchen garden. Such a box (sold at plant stores) comes in various lengths, in wood or plastic, and fits on the sill or is attached with L-shaped brackets at the bottom of the window. Plant directly into soil in the box, or, even easier, set containers inside the box. A window box 3 feet long will hold about a dozen plants.

Before leaving the kitchen, do not overlook the area's adjoining "rooms" (pantries and alcoves). Here you can fuss over plants to your heart's content and not bother anyone.

Bathrooms

Bathrooms are one of the most ideal spot for vegetables (or any plant) because of the humidity from showers and baths. And being rather sterile, the bathroom is spruced up with the addition of greenery. As with the kitchen, the window is the perfect place for your plants (and the plants will effectively serve as a "curtain," providing some necessary privacy). Use the same shelf setup in the bathroom as you use in the kitchen. You can also install shelves on the bathroom walls, which is a perfect solution if your bathroom lacks a window. Supplement with artificial light in such a situation.

Window Greenhouses

Vegetables thrive in window greenhouses, whether self-made or the commercially manufactured units. The advantage of making your own window greenhouse is that it will be custom-fitted for your existing window; you will not have to remove the window first, as is often necessary with commercial units.

Herbs especially like growing in a window greenhouse. A standard window greenhouse will hold 20 to 30 plants, and adds a decorative touch to whatever room it is in, from kitchen to bathroom to pantry, den, or family room. Growing conditions are practically perfect in this setup because ample humidity and excellent light are supplied to the vegetables if the greenhouse is the type that opens. With the closed unit, install a small fan and run it at low speed to keep air circulating all the

Acrylic Window Greenhouse

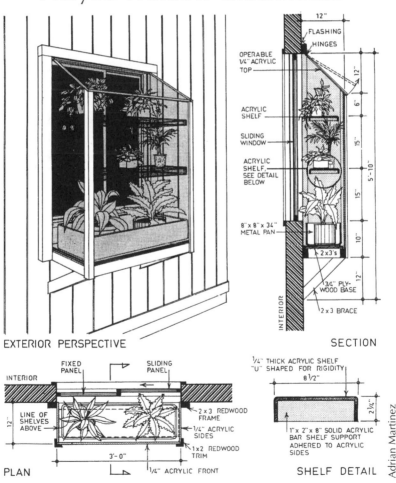

EXTERIOR PERSPECTIVE

SECTION

12"
FLASHING
HINGES
OPERABLE 1/4" ACRYLIC TOP
ACRYLIC SHELF
SLIDING WINDOW
ACRYLIC SHELF, SEE DETAIL BELOW
8" x 8" x 34" METAL PAN
2 x 3's
3/4" PLYWOOD BASE
2 x 3 BRACE
INTERIOR
12"
6"
15"
5'-10"
15"
10"
12"

PLAN

FIXED PANEL
SLIDING PANEL
INTERIOR
LINE OF SHELVES ABOVE
2 x 3 REDWOOD FRAME
1/4" ACRYLIC SIDES
1 x 2 REDWOOD TRIM
1/4" ACRYLIC FRONT
3'-0"
12"

SHELF DETAIL

1/4" THICK ACRYLIC SHELF "U" SHAPED FOR RIGIDITY
8 1/2"
2 1/4"
1" x 2" x 8" SOLID ACRYLIC BAR SHELF SUPPORT ADHERED TO ACRYLIC SIDES

Adrian Martinez

18

time (replace the fan with a space heater in cold-winter areas).

I have made several window greenhouses from ¹/₄-inch-thick acrylic plastic. Commercially made units come in wood and glass combinations, and you assemble all the pieces according to the instructions. Another type of manufactured greenhouse is a bubble of one-piece molded clear plastic.

Table Greenhouses

Table greenhouses are usually made of plastic. Most of these small, freestanding units are too small for growing vegetables unless they are 24 inches wide by 60 inches long. They will hold 12 good-sized plants. You can use the other, smaller units, however, to start vegetable seeds or grow small herbs.

Sunrooms

Sunrooms are ideal for vegetables. Because these rooms are mainly windows, light is no problem. Planter boxes and bins and window shelves are ideal for these areas. A sunroom is also a great place for relaxing over coffee and puttering with plants. A spare room or porch can be converted into a sunroom.

Plant Rooms

A plant room, unlike a sunroom, is for plants only. The room is similar to a solarium, with lots of glass and top light, usually in the form of a clerestory window or skylight. A water outlet is essential in the plant room, and you may want to extend heating ducts from the home to furnish heat. Growing many plants in a plant room creates a system of humidity.

Hanging Plants

Certain vegetables, such as lettuce and tomatoes, do especially well when grown suspended in hanging containers, and such containers adapt to any room or spot in the home. Besides getting sufficient light, hanging plants get air circulating all around them.

Make sure each hanging container has an attached saucer to catch water. The plastic pots are sold with the saucer attached; with terra cotta pots, you will have to buy separate saucers and attach them to the pots with triangular wire clip-ons.

Don't hang plants too high or too low—you want a level that is convenient for watering, and you do not want plants so low that they interfere with people traffic. Remember that hanging vegetables need more water (daily) than plants in a window greenhouse because of the air circulating all around them. Use a long-nosed watering can.

I do not recommend suspending a container with macramé because the material usually rots within a year. To ensure that the container is securely fastened to the ceiling, screw an S-hook or a screw eye into a wood joist (use a stud finder to determine where the joist is). Hang containers with a strong chain; some pots can weigh more than 25 pounds. Do not use monofilament wire because it is not strong enough for heavy weights.

Living Rooms and Dining Rooms

I mentioned that I do not like the appearance of food plants growing in these rooms. If you want to have vegetables in these areas, however, grow them in hanging containers and have just one or two large containers in the rooms in scale with the rooms' furnishings. Remember that because the windows in these areas are usually covered with curtains, blinds, or shutters, light is not at its best. Also, these rooms are usually dry, lacking the humidity vegetables need. Be careful when watering plants to avoid staining carpets with water and/or soil.

CHAPTER 3

Basics of Growing Food Plants

The ABCs of vegetable growing involve soil, light, air, water, feeding, and protection from insects and disease. Careful attention to each detail will provide you with a bounty of produce.

SOIL

Nonfood plants can survive without perfect soil because they do not have to produce a harvest, but vegetables demand a balanced and nutritional soil. Without such soil, they simply will not bear properly.

Soil is available in sacks, by the bushel, and by the truckload. Sacks of soil are sold by quarts: 5, 10, and so on. Your selection of the weight will depend on how much soil you need and how much you can easily and comfortably handle. Also, consider where you live and the space you have: You do not want to lug lots of soil up the stairs or in the elevator if you live in a high-rise, not to mention the fact that you will not have the room to store much soil.

All forms of soil have been screened to eliminate rock and debris; some soils have compost added, some contain fertilizer, and some contain fillers, namely, sawdust. The soil for your vegetables should be rich and friable. A rich soil is high in organic matter or microorganisms that transform chemical matter into food for the plant. Friable soil allows air to circulate through it. Air must enter soil so the soil can carry water to the roots of the plant. Crops such as carrots have roots that have to bear into the soil; they cannot if the soil is hard and cakey. A carrot that has to struggle to penetrate the soil will develop fiber; the more fiber, the less sugar is produced.

Vegetables also need a soil that contains compost (decayed vegetable matter), which increases friability and loosens the soil's structure. Nurseries and other outlets sell compost or manure in sacks; you add the material to the soil. Also, do not overlook nitrogen, which is necessary for good plant growth. Add nitrogen food to packaged soil. Bonemeal, cottonseed meal, and blood meal (sold in sacks at nurseries) all contain a high percentage of nitrogen.

Packaged Soil

A packaged soil mix technically has everything you need in a soil, but you still should add to it, as just mentioned. Many packaged soil mixes already exist for fruit trees, vegetables, houseplants, and others. It is impossible to know everything that is in a packaged mix, and the manufacturers are under no obligation to list the ingredients. Also, you cannot open a bag of soil in the store to feel it; your best bet is to squeeze the bag: If it feels loose and is fairly dark in color, it is okay. If it feels hard and grainy, it is not worth buying.

22

Loose Soil and Soil-less Mixes

The advantage of buying loose soil by the bushel is that you can run your hand through it. The soil should feel mealy, like a well-done baked potato, smell fresh and earthy, and look rich brown in color. The soil-less mixes are fine for some vegetables such as tomatoes and peppers because they eliminate the danger of root nematode and some soil-borne diseases. But if you use these mixes, you must fertilize regularly so plants receive sufficient amounts of food.

LIGHT AND AIR

All plants need light if they are to grow and prosper. Light is necessary for the process of photosynthesis, in which light transforms a plant's chemical elements into food for that plant. Certain vegetables, such as tomatoes, need more light than root crops, such as carrots and radishes.

Leafy vegetables can withstand low levels of light, but even they need ample light if no sun is available. Summer light of course is brighter than winter light, and plants are quite sensitive to this difference in intensity. If you are growing seedlings indoors during the winter it is a good idea to supplement the weaker natural light with artificial light from an incandescent lamp.

Vegetables also demand a fresh circulation of air. Outdoors, nature furnishes sufficient air, but indoors you may need to run a small fan at low speed to supply air circulation on those stagnant summer days.

WATERING

Vegetables must be watered heavily because wetting only part of the soil will leave pockets of dryness where roots cannot get water. Every particle of the soil must have water so food can be carried to the plants. Without the right amount of water, vegetables will produce a sparse harvest. These plants are on a liquid diet; water is their lifeline.

23

Although it is important to keep the soil moist, it is equally important that you not drown the vegetables. Try to keep the soil evenly moist so the plants can get the oxygen they need to maintain healthy growth.

Drip Watering

Watering with a hose results in pockets of wet and dry soil. Not all the roots receive water, and so they will grow in other directions, seeking water. With sprinklers, water is delivered away from rather than on plants. Most of the water evaporates in the air and runs off the surface of the soil. Also, the water pressure fluctuates with a sprinkler.

Drip irrigation is the frequent application of water to plant roots only, through emitters (holes) located at selected points along plastic water delivery lines. The lines are small in diameter and installed on the surface of the soil; the water seeps through the holes in the lines to the soil below. Hardware stores and nurseries sell various drip systems in kits. You can also buy the separate parts and assemble the parts yourself. Some drip system manufacturers also offer misting and sprinkler emitters that deposit water directly on plants, not around it, as regular sprinklers do.

Be sure you do not overload the setup—too many emitters in a system will not work efficiently because the regulated and steady flow of water will be interrupted. (The instructions in the kits will give you this information.) Also, the water must be filtered of sediment, soil, and mineral deposits so it does not clog the emitters. Most drip systems have a filter unit that removes particles that might clog the workings of the hoses.

Study the drawings within this book to help select and set up your own drip watering system. I heartily recommend such a system, which is a blessing.

24

Types of Emitters

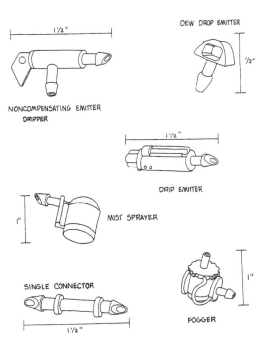

Michael Valdez

FEEDING

Vegetables need the elements nitrogen, phosphorus, and potassium to grow well. The plants use up the elements quickly, so they must be replenished via the process known as feeding.

Plant foods come in liquid, soluble, and granule form. The soluble plant foods are mixed with water; granular plant foods are scattered on the soil, and then water is added. Liquid plant food is the best form for vegetables; it comes in many strengths, as indicated on the bottle. For example, 10-10-5 or 20-20-10 denotes the percentage of nitrogen, phosphorous, and potassium in that order. Use a 20-20-5 solution for leafy vegetables, 10-20-10 for root crops such as carrots and beets, and the all-purpose 10-10-5 for other vegetables.

Overfeeding can kill vegetables; use a weak solution every other watering during the growing season. After you transplant seedlings, start feeding and continue doing so regularly.

Remember that you must keep the soil evenly moist. Feeding alone does not make plants grow; they also need even moisture at their roots. Follow these four rules for successful feeding of vegetables:

1. Never feed plants in caked soil; water the soil first.
2. Never feed vegetables in the hot midday sun.
3. Never feed ailing plants hoping that this will make them grow.
4. Never overfeed; if you miss an application, wait for the next regularly scheduled application.

GROWING VEGETABLES
UNDER ARTIFICIAL LIGHT

Artificial light—fluorescent, incandescent, or halogen—enables you to grow vegetables in out-of-the way spots that receive little if any natural light, such as basements, closets, and pantries. Fluorescent light is the most popular kind for growing plants. Fluorescent lamps for this purpose are sold under various brand names. The everyday warm- to cool-white fluorescent bulbs used in factories and homes for overall illumination are also fine for vegetables. Artificial light can be the sole source of light for your plants, or you can use it in combination with any natural light. Fluorescent bulbs last about 12 months.

The commercially made setups are available in table models and floor units. You can make your own display with a fluorescent light bulb attached to the underside of a kitchen cabinet or install four lamps at the top of a window. The best results will be attained with two 40-watt lamps with a reflector, which will supply 800- to 900-foot candles, the amount that root vegetables and leafy ones prefer. The lamps are available in lengths of 18 to 72 inches. To grow many foodstuffs, four lamps for every 4 square feet of space is the recommended amount of light.

Incandescent lights (the kind you use for reading) are also fine for growing plants. A combination lamp, incorporating both fluorescent and incandescent light, is now available as well. The plant lamp can be installed in standard light sockets.

Grow your plants on a waist-high table, dresser, or other support. Buy a standard reflector fixture at a supply house and mount it 12 to 16 inches above the table or other surface by suspending it with chain that is securely fastened to the ceiling (install hooks in ceiling joists). This standard fixture will hold two or four fluorescent bulbs. Garden centers sell commercially made table units that come with two lamps, a stand, and a tray (more sophisticated models are also sold at the centers).

If the table or other flat surface is underneath a cabinet, attach a strip fluorescent fixture to the bottom of the cabinet. To use a closet as the growing area, build shelves in the closet. Paint the shelves white on all sides for maximum reflection of light. Then attach lamps to the undersides of the shelves.

Leave lamps on 12 to 14 hours a day. Any natural light combined with artificial light will be even better for the vegetables. Remember to give your vegetables short periods of darkness; an automatic timer is the best way to shut off the lamps so you do not have to remember to do it yourself.

Plants under light grow all the time, so they need more water than plants growing naturally. Keep soil evenly moist; provide good ventilation or insects will attack your plants. A

26

small fan going at low speed is the best way to provide the proper flow of air. Keep humidity at 50 percent; anything higher may lead to fungus diseases. A hygrometer measures humidity and can be purchased at a hardware store.

Plants growing under artificial light need more feeding than other plants. Feed at every other watering, but do not overfeed. Keep daytime temperatures at 68° to 74° Fahrenheit; a 10° drop at night is okay. If insects invade the vegetables, follow the guidelines in chapter 10 for getting rid of them.

Germinating seeds under artificial light is the ideal way to start vegetables. The best arrangement is a two-lamp cool-white fluorescent bulb in combination with four 8-watt incandescent lamps. The blend of artificial light accelerates germination and growth. Place pans or trays 3 to 4 inches from the light; keep lights on 14 to 16 hours. When seeds have germinated, keep seedlings 10 inches from the lamps; again, keep lights on 16 hours.

CHAPTER 4

Containers for Vegetables

By growing vegetables in containers, you control what soil is being used, prevent insects from becoming a problem when plants are grown in the ground, position plants where you want them, and somewhat decrease how far you have to bend to tend plants. There is a host of small to large containers you can use, from wood boxes and planters to clay pots, wine kegs, and hanging baskets. Some types of containers can be placed on dollies, enabling you to easily wheel the containers from spot to spot. Whether you buy them or build them yourself, you will find an array of containers for your vegetables.

WOOD CONTAINERS

Wood is the easiest material to use when making containers such as boxes and planters. The wood container can be used indoors or outdoors. Boxes that have a finished appearance, such as those with moldings, are best indoors. Drip saucers or trays will be necessary to catch excess water for any indoor container. These may be standard clay saucers, acrylic dishes, or even pie plates.

Vegetable Containers

Michael Valdez

Boxes

A wood box for a plant may be elaborate or simple in design; it may have outside detailing or be perfectly plain. The plan of the box can vary too. It may have overlapped corners or crossed timbers, be spiral in shape or octagonal, and so forth.

Boxes for plants are popular and easy and cheap to make. The box can be large or small, square, rectangular, or circular—the size and shape depend on your imagination. The most simple box has four sides and a bottom with drainage holes. What's more, you can merely nail a box together, but a combination of glue and screws makes a box last longer. Use brass screws and good-quality glue or epoxy. For small boxes, 1-inch lumber is fine; for large boxes, use 2-inch stock.

Redwood Window Planter

30

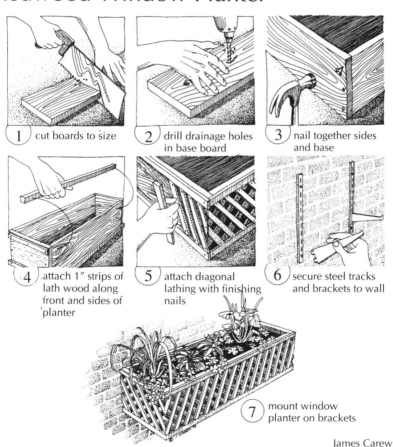

1. cut boards to size
2. drill drainage holes in base board
3. nail together sides and base
4. attach 1" strips of lath wood along front and sides of planter
5. attach diagonal lathing with finishing nails
6. secure steel tracks and brackets to wall
7. mount window planter on brackets

James Carew

A standard 16 x 20 inch rectangular box is 5 inches deep and made of redwood. It is suitable for almost any small planting. Nail small chunks of wood under each bottom corner to elevate the box slightly. Another type of box, the cube, is neat and simple. For a ¹/₂-inch cube, use 1 x 1 ¹/₂ inch strips of redwood. Screw and glue together the four sides and the bottom, and then add some wooden 2 x 2 inch moldings at the top and edges to give the box character (see p. 33 for an illustration of molding). Run the edge moldings vertically to define the box.

On boxes you can make other refinements, such as spacing the slats ¹/₂ inch apart, tacking trelliswork onto the face of the box, or, if you are highly imaginative, scoring the box with a simple design to give it dimension. You can also taper the box and bevel (angle-cut) the corners and use a plywood base for a more finished appearance. As you will see, there are innumerable ways to make a box more than a box.

Planters

Planters, contrasted with boxes, are wooden boxes that are longer and narrower or of window box shape. The design of the planter requires some thought: small planters coordinate with small plants, large ones with large plants.

Planters can be used at floor or ground level, and indoors (built-in planters) or outdoors (on patios and decks). Outdoors, planters should be elevated with 2-inch blocks under each corner so air can enter the box from underneath and thus eliminate hiding places for insects. In the home, planters should be raised for maximum good looks.

Indoors, the planter is basically used to define a long space: in a stairwell, along a window, or as a room divider. The indoor planter must be made from kiln-dried wood and should have a galvanized-metal insert and some drainage facilities. Have a sheet-metal shop make the insert, and have them put in a spigot.

For the best look, paint planters white or a neutral color. Also, design and motif are most important for indoor planters. The indoor planter is perhaps the most difficult container to make properly because it needs careful craftsmanship and good finishing touches to be totally handsome in a room.

Outdoor planters are easy to make (usually just four sides and a bottom) and can be built from construction-grade redwood. They need not be painted, and if they are made of redwood they will eventually turn a lovely silver color. For finishing touches, use moldings or caps at the tops. Make outdoor planters from 2 x 4 inch or 2 x 12 inch lumber. A good size is 12 inches wide, 10 inches deep, and 36 inches long. (Of course, you can alter this size to your specific needs and the vegetables you want to grow.) Large plants will, by necessity, need large planters, though small plants can be accommodated in 1 12- or 1 6-inch box.

Handsome square molding stacking, stacked, lined up, and so forth, can be used outdoors in varying plans to create a total container garden. A practical size is 20 x 20 inches. Indoors, the modular planter does not look handsome, since it takes up too much space and for some reason seems incongruous with home furnishings.

Built-in Planters

The built-in planter was popular in the 1930s and is making a comeback. These planters are room dividers, stair railings, windowsills, racks, or accent "islands" near stairwells. Properly made and built with some imagination, built-in planters are very attractive, but made improperly and put in an unsuitable location they can be ugly.

Built-in indoor planters require a good hand at carpentry and excellent finishing work—painting, sanding, and so forth. Such planters also need galvanized bin inserts for the plants, which can be costly. If you have little space for plants in your home, the built-in planter is the answer, because you can grow many plants in otherwise unused space.

The interior windowsill planter is a terrific one to build; it looks good and works beautifully because it is near the window, thereby giving your plants sufficient light. The planter in a bookcase or used as a room divider is not as successful, although if you use low-light-type plants, they will probably survive in such cases.

Before you embark on a built-in planter project, consider all the factors: Is there enough light for the plants? Will the material used match the existing woodwork? What will the total cost be?

Window Boxes

Window boxes are popular in Europe, but in the United States, unfortunately, they are not used as much as they could be. The window box is actually a very effective way of having some tiny vegetables or herbs even if you live in an apartment. The drawbacks are that in winter the box must be covered and looks bleak. It also may not be permitted in an apartment building, but window box greenery does a lot to make some gardening possible in the city.

Nurseries sell plastic or wood window boxes, but these are not usually aesthetically handsome or the correct size. You are better off making your own window box with either redwood or cedar, at least 1 inch thick, and a plywood (³/₄-inch) base. Regardless of the design you decide on, make the window box at least 10 inches wide and 10 inches deep to allow enough root room for the plants. Drill drainage holes in the bottom of the box every 8 inches.

Window Box

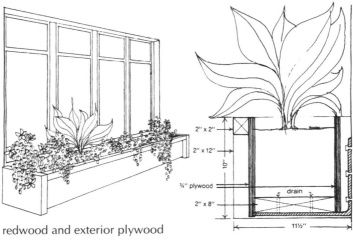

redwood and exterior plywood

Adrian Martinez

The window box can be a simple rectangle with straight sides; or, if you live in severe winter climates, consider a box that has a slope-outward edge. This type of window box lets soil expand when it is frozen—without damaging the box.

Attaching the box to the window is more difficult than actually making the box. Use metal L-shaped brackets for support under the box. To strongly secure the box to the house wall, use screws, lag bolts, or toggle bolts.

Working with Wood

Many handcrafted containers are made from wood. Wood is easy to work with, and you do not have to be a carpenter or be very handy with tools. In fact, if you don't want to do any cutting or sawing at home, you can order (for a slight cost) all wood pieces for the design you've made cut to size. Then all you have to do is nail, screw, or glue the parts together to make your boxes, planters, or other containers. Make sure you have the proper tools and know something about adhesives and wood epoxies (we will give you information about tools and these materials later in this chapter).

What to Know about Wood

The basic wood for containers is either redwood or cedar, because these woods resist weathering. For outdoor use, construction-grade redwood—that is, redwood with a few slight defects—is fine. For indoor use, purchase kiln-dried redwood or cedar; this wood is blemish-free and smooth to the touch. Indoors and outdoors you can also use pine or Douglas fir—if you protect the wood with preservatives or paint. (There are many preservative-coating products at paint stores.)

If you do not want to cut the wood for your container at home, tell the lumber dealer the dimensions of the boards or pieces you need, and he will cut the wood for you. There are a few fundamentals about ordering wood that you should know, if you don't already. Order wood first by thickness, width, and length; for example, 2 inches thick x 6 inches wide x 8 feet long. Next, specify what type of wood you want, such as redwood, and then you indicate the grade, such as construction-grade, kiln-dried, rough, or smooth. Bear in mind that if you order standard 2 x 4 inch boards, the *actual* dimensions of the board will be 1 ¹/₂ x 3 ¹/₂ or slightly larger. In other words, the boards will never be exactly 2 x 4. Pieces of wood smaller than 2 x 4 inches are referred to as "strips." You would call these strips, 2 x 3's or 1 x 2's, for example. Also, you should be aware that posts for corner construction are either 4 inches or 2 inches square.

Detailing Containers

No matter what kind of wood container you are making, if the bare look of wood is not to your liking, you can easily alter it by various detailing methods.

With a little extra time and not much more money, wood containers can be handsomely detailed on the outside. You can use wood strips to form such outside designs as lattice-work and diamond patterns. The detailing puts the finishing touches on the containers and adds a note of elegance.

A simple but effective outside-the-container motif is a raised rectangle outlining the container, which creates a shadowbox effect. For the average container this requires sixteen pieces of 1 x 2 inch strips of wood. Another method is to place strips of wood vertically or horizontally a ¹/₂ inch apart; this will add flair to the basic box as well as cover any construction mistakes.

When you detail a wood container, you should always add a molding (or cap) at the top to give it finish and add dimension. Caps are usually 1 x 3 inches; nail them in place, letting the outer edge overhang the container by ¹/₂ to 1 inch.

You do not need extensive tools to make wood containers. You will, however, need a good hammer. I prefer the claw hammer or forged, high-quality steel. Hammer faces, or heads, are flat or slightly convex; the convex hammer, which lets you drive a nail flush without marring wood surfaces, is the best one for your purposes. Longhandled hammers provide more leverage than short ones and are more suitable for framing work, but an average-sized handle will give you plenty of leverage for the standard container—even a container that is 24 inches square. Also, it is a good idea to have a shorthandled hammer for the finishing work. The head of this hammer should weigh about 16 ounces.

The screwdriver is an important tool because containers last longer if they are screwed together. Buy three basic screwdrivers: a screwdriver with a square shank; a long screwdriver, which gives you more leverage than a short one; and a small screwdriver for working in tight places like corners. An ill-fitting screwdriver can give you a headache. If the tip is too large for the screw's heads, for example, the screwdriver will mar the surface of the wood.

You can also now buy magnetized screwdrivers, which greatly reduce the possibility of the screwdriver tip slipping from the screw head.

If you are building a wood container, you will certainly need a handsaw (a power saw is not really necessary). The shape, number of teeth, and blade size determine the type of cutting a saw will do. The crosscut saw is probably the most popular; this saw is made to cut across the wood grain, and it can cut both plywood and hardwoods. A 20-inch saw and smaller saw for detail work are basically all you need for making containers. If you are cutting patterns, use what is called a coping saw.

For outside detailing or scoring, you will need chisels. Chisels make small grooves and cuts in the wood. Most of them are driven with a hammer. A set of four chisels in blade widths of $^1/_4$, $^1/_2$, $^3/_4$, and 1 inch is fine. When you are doing chisel work, use light taps with the hammer, and remove the wood in small stages one step at a time.

The Miter Box

Moldings cover many mistakes, and most boxes look best when capped with a molding. The best tool for making moldings is a miter box. With thin, inexpensive gadgets you can cut precise 45° angles needed for joining moldings together. The miter box comes with a 45°-angle saw slot. Apply the wood molding against the framing edge, and with a hacksaw (square-type saw) make your cuts—an easy, effectual way of cutting precisely and accurately.

Nails

There are so many different types of nails that you should carefully look over the selection at our hardware store. The right nail for the right job is important. Ordinary nails come in bright and galvanized finishes and are designated as box, casing, common, or scaffold nails. For your purposes the common nail is satisfactory, although the box nail is somewhat better because it is less likely to split the wood. For finishing work use the finishing, or casing, nail.

Standard box and casing nails come in sizes from 2-penny to 16-penny. Years ago, the term "penny" meant the cost of a hundred nails—a hundred of the *smallest* nails cost two pennies. Today, the term indicates the length of the nail.

Glues and Epoxies

Wood glues and epoxies come in such a wide variety that it's enough to confuse the average buyer. Glue applied at the corners of containers adds strength, and epoxy holds joints together practically forever.

Animal or fish glues are most satisfactory when making indoor containers, where the temperature and humidity do not vary widely. A white glue known as polyvinyl glue is also used in making containers, but for a very strong waterproof joint you will need a resorcin resin. This is one of the most durable glues for outdoor-container usage. You must mix the powdered catalyst with liquid resin; then you have about 10 minutes to form the joint after mixing the glue. Ask your hardware store for particulars.

Epoxies for wood are also generally easy to use. Drying time varies for these adhesives, and clamps may be necessary to hold the wood pieces together until the epoxy sets. Again, ask your hardware dealer for advice on the best one for the job.

No matter what kind of adhesive you use for bonding joints, be sure to ask for one that is waterproof.

Finishes and Paints

You can use any number of clear sealants and paints to finish containers. The paint or clear finish protects them, with or even without their being detailed. And each, by the way, has their own beauty. Some people say the unadorned box is more natural and more handsome than an embellished one. This is a matter of taste. I have seen beautiful detailed or painted boxes, and I have also seen many fine examples of natural boxes applied with merely clear-sealant finishes.

There are numerous types of finishes on the market under different trade names, and it is therefore difficult to recommend a specific brand. A clear, tough finish is what you want; also, ask your paint dealer for a wood finish that dries quickly.

A finish protects the wood container and at the same time gives it a lustrous appearance. With any finish the trick is to brush it on evenly and smoothly. You can use one or two coats. It is a simple operation and goes a long way in protecting the wood from wear.

You can also achieve a clear finish by using waxes on unfinished wood; the build up of wax creates a protective finish that is handsome and lustrous. Various types of waxes are available at paint and hardware stores. Consult the dealer about what to use to achieve the type of finish you want.

An infinite number of types of paint can be used on wood containers, and just what you select depends on your personal tastes. In any case, wood containers and wood housings should be sanded smooth before you apply the paint. Also, if the container is to be used outside, you will want outdoor-type paints. Indoors you may use enamels.

OTHER CONTAINERS

Terra Cotta and Plastic Pots

The advantage of terra cotta is that the material dries out quickly; thus the soil also dries out quickly, preventing overwatering and stagnant soil conditions. The natural terra cotta color also blends well with the outdoors.

Terra cotta pots are available in very small to very large sizes (48 inches in diameter). The 30-inch-diameter pot is the average size for most vegetables. Unglazed pots cost much less than the newer glazed Italian-, Venetian-, and Spanish-style terra cotta pots. Glazed pots come in several colors but often do not have drainage holes (these pots are frequently used as cache-pots for houseplants), so be sure to check a glazed pot before buying one—without the proper drainage, the soil will become waterlogged, and the vegetables will not prosper. Also, if you use the glazed pots, be sure to soak them well with a hose so they do not absorb the water from the soil the vegetables need.

Flexible or rigid plastic pots are lightweight and available in many colors, shapes, and sizes (up to 40 inches in diameter). The flexible plastic containers are not very attractive or durable; use the rigid plastic (acrylic) pots.

Some gardeners prefer plastic pots because they are easy to clean and hold water longer than terra cotta pots, so plants in them need less frequent watering. Never lift a filled pot by its rim or the container may crack from the weight of the soil.

Casks, Barrels, and Kegs

Casks, barrels, and kegs are ideal for vegetables because of their size (36 inches in diameter) and rustic look, which is so appropriate outdoors. Nurseries, supermarkets, and other stores sell the sawed-in-half containers, usually at a fairly inexpensive price. Be sure the cask, barrel, or keg has galvanized bands around it to keep staves in place, otherwise the staves will loosen after a while. Squash, cucumbers, and green peppers do fine in these containers.

Garbage Cans and Vegetable Crocks

Yes, even garbage cans are suitable for vegetables. The containers are available in nonbendable, heavy-duty plastic, in sizes from 10 gallons up, and in colors including green and brown, which look good outdoors. They are perfect for vegetables because they are wide and quite deep. A good garbage can costs about $20.

You can find old vegetable crocks in thrift shops and secondhand furniture stores. These blue-glazed crocks are used for making sauerkraut and other dishes. Some crocks come in very large sizes; drill drainage holes with a drill and bit. The crocks are quite handsome when brimming with vegetables.

Hanging Containers

Hanging slatted wood containers, acrylic boxes, and wire baskets are all ideal for growing vegetables, especially lettuce and dwarf tomatoes. The containers can be suspended from deck or balcony rafters, patio overhangs, and even doorways. Hanging plants do well because both air and light will reach all parts of the plants. Be sure all hanging containers are securely fastened to a support and at a height that enables you to reach the plants for easy watering and grooming. Also be sure the containers have attached saucers to catch excess water (hanging in the air, vegetables will need tons of water).

The most popular wood hanging container is the cross-hatched basket. A simple square or rectangular frame with an opening for a pot and saucer is also attractive. The standard acrylic box is rectangular in shape, with a round cutout for a pot. The acrylic disk consists of circles strung together with monofilament wire. Each disk can hold one potted plant; the weight of the pot steadies the tray. You can buy wire baskets or make your own. Cut the wire with wire snips and weave or solder the pieces together.

Discarded Containers and Homemade Planters

Some garden experts feel that vegetables do not do as well in salvaged or homemade containers as they do in terra cotta pots. This is definitely untrue. As long as you properly water your plants in these containers, plants will thrive. Vases and stone troughs are fine for seedlings and larger vegetable plants. Even ice cream cartons, which will not last more than 6 months, are fine until that time.

Cans

One- or two-pound coffee cans are ideal for vegetables. Use the plastic lids as saucers for catching water. Cover up the brand name with contact paper or paint the can. Punch drainage holes in the bottom of the can. Other ideal cans are Crisco cans, peanut tins, cracker cans, and round cookie tins. Wash all cans thoroughly; put in some gravel, charcoal chips, soil, and then the vegetable plants.

Plastic Containers, Bottles, and Jugs

Cottage cheese and margarine containers are fine for seeds; plastic detergent and bleach jugs are perfect for larger vegetable plants. To use the jugs, cut them midway, making an 8-inch tub. Be sure to punch in some drainage holes. You can decorate all these containers with colored tape.

Buy an inexpensive glass-cutter kit and cut off cider jugs, wine bottles, pickle jars, and other glass containers halfway. Take the containers to a glass store and have them drill drainage holes in the bottoms.

Coffee-Can Plant Housing

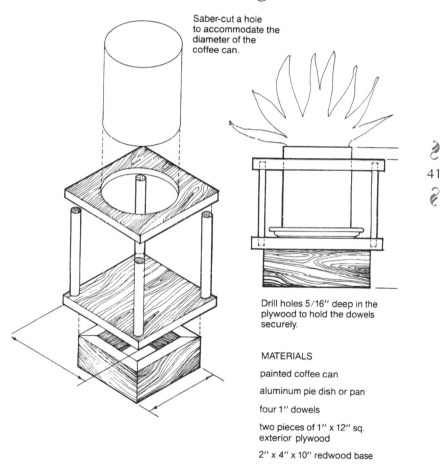

Saber-cut a hole to accommodate the diameter of the coffee can.

41

Drill holes 5/16″ deep in the plywood to hold the dowels securely.

MATERIALS

painted coffee can

aluminum pie dish or pan

four 1″ dowels

two pieces of 1″ x 12″ sq. exterior plywood

2″ x 4″ x 10″ redwood base

Adrian Martinez

Display Units

Plant Stands

Today, plant stands, platforms, and trolleys are available for displaying your vegetables. By elevating plants, you actually help them grow better because air will reach underneath the unit, getting to plants' roots. As long as you use a drip pan on the display unit, no water will drip onto the carpet or floor.

A single plant stand is called a pedestal—a small, high table that is circular, square, or rectangular and made of either wood, mirrored title, or acrylic. A plant stand can also be a wood cube or rectangle with brass tiles, Mylar, or reflective contact paper cemented or adhered to it. To make an acrylic plant stand, buy a 10-inch-high cylinder from a plastics supplier and glue a circular top on it.

When designing and making a plant stand, be sure to keep it simple and of a size in proportion to its surroundings. For example, a tall (60 inches) plant stand looks good in a corner; a smaller stand, such as 36 inches, looks better near a window. If you make the stand from wood, use kiln-dried redwood for interior stands and construction-grade wood for outside stands.

You can also buy metal plant stands that have arms that hold plants on small trays as well as tension-pole stands equipped with plant trays. An inexpensive multiplant stand can be constructed from an acrylic tube or iron pipe outfitted with supports or trays.

Platforms

Many people put their plants directly on the floor or right on tables. This practice leads to water stains, but plants are displayed to their fullest advantage. You can make a handsome platform from acrylic with a topless box that is 10 inches long, 8 inches wide, and 2 inches deep, and then cover it with redwood slats. Put gravel into the box to catch excess water.

Even easier to construct is a wood box platform; put gravel or sphagnum moss in the box for absorbing excess water. Circular platforms of acrylic or wooden rounds are also charming.

Trolleys

These dollies are wood platforms with wheels, making it easy to move larger plants. The trolley can be round or square. You can also buy dollies at nurseries, which are tubs with wheels.

Drip Trays

Any plant container used indoors needs a drip tray (saucer or pan) to prevent excess water from dripping onto the floor or furniture. Use terra cotta saucers, large pie plates, or trays made of galvanized metal. See the drawing for more details. Of course, the size of the saucer will depend on the size of the container.

Drip Pans

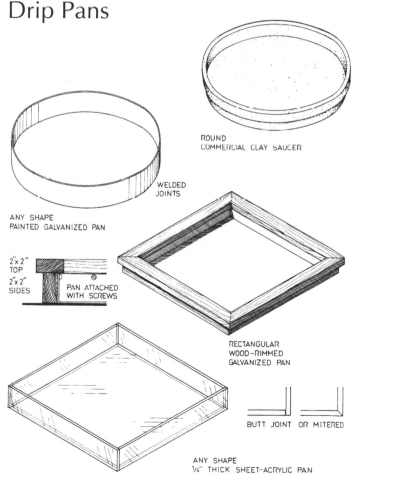

ROUND
COMMERCIAL CLAY SAUCER

WELDED
JOINTS

ANY SHAPE
PAINTED GALVANIZED PAN

2"x 2"
TOP
2"x 2"
SIDES

PAN ATTACHED
WITH SCREWS

RECTANGULAR
WOOD-RIMMED
GALVANIZED PAN

BUTT JOINT OR MITERED

ANY SHAPE
¼" THICK SHEET-ACRYLIC PAN

43

Adrian Martinez

Tiles

Floor or mosaic tiles, in 6-inch squares, come in many designs and colors. Five tiles used together will make a pretty container. You can cement together the five pieces of tile: four tiles for the sides and one for the bottom. However, I suggest you use a $1/2$-inch-thick plywood base instead, because it is much easier to drill drainage holes in wood than in tile, and the plywood base will not detract from the appearance of the container.

Use a flat working surface, such as a table or bench, and protect the surface with newspaper or wax paper. Apply a ribbon of ceramic epoxy (purchased at tile outlets) along the edges of the tiles. Secure the pieces while the cement sets by using strips of masking tape at each corner.

Tile Sewer Pipes and Flues

Sewer or drain pipes and flues, in tile or rigid plastic, are available at building supply yards. Sizes and shapes are as varied as sewer connections, but believe me, there is a large world of plant containers to make from these inexpensive and attractive materials.

The regular double-hub 4-inch tile flue or pipe is terra cotta in color and makes an original, attractive container. Outdoors, set the pipe on the ground, fill it with soil, and plant. Indoors, you'll need a $1/4$-inch plywood base for the pipe. Other clay pipes, in diameters of 4, 5, or 6 inches, are called *straight* cylinders (without the hub caps) and can also be used as is for pedestals, for outdoor planting, or, with a base, for attractive indoor plant containers.

The rigid plastic pipe available in various diameters comes in black or white and can be used in the same manner as clay pipes. Plastic has a sophisticated look that compliments many home interiors.

Concrete Blocks

Hollow-core concrete blocks can be found at lumberyards, and it is worth a trip there to find them, because they are inexpensive and make fine outdoor plant housings. The blocks come in several sizes, usually 12 x 8 x 12 inches or 12 x 8 x 16 inches.

They are set on the ground, filled with soil, and then can be planted. If you group several together, you can create a handsome container garden in a short time. You can also stack blocks one on top of the other for more planting depth. Concrete blocks lend themselves to many modular designs for patios or garden, and their natural gray color usually harmonizes well with outdoor furniture.

Kitchenwire Baskets

There are numerous types of kitchenwire baskets available at shops, and people are using them effectively for plants rather than kitchen uses. Sometimes called lettuce baskets, these items require careful planning to become a satisfactory housing for hanging plants. Wire baskets may also be used to hold lettuce or other leafy greens.

Washtubs, Nail Kegs, and Wine Barrels

When you think of a tub for a plant, a washtub immediately comes to mind. These make fine containers for some vegetables such as dwarf tomatoes and cucumbers. Punch drain holes in the bottom of the tub. Other tubs suitable for plants are empty steel drums or rigid, plastic-coated, five-gallon ice-cream containers. However, ice-cream tubs are merely temporary because they are only made of heavy-duty cardboard. Eventually water will rot them.

Nail kegs and small wine barrels are sturdier ready-made tubs that need little modification to make them ideal for edible plants. You'll find that most barrels are already sawed in half at the midpoint; but if you get a barrel from a winery, it is easy to saw it yourself. Make a chalk mark around the belly of the barrel and saw along the mark. Shallow barrel halves or ends filled with vegetables look charmingly old-fashioned on patios and porches. Or you may saw the kegs or barrels in half lengthwise and fit them with pipes as legs; you will thereby have two long, shallow planters. Of course, you may use the barrels uncut, if you find them so and desire the additional height.

Nail kegs and barrels come in several sizes. The 12- and 18-inch depths are the most suitable for many plants. Look for barrels or kegs that have galvanized hoops; those with black iron hoops must be painted or they will rust. (To locate barrels and kegs, look in the yellow pages.) Remember, too, to drill drainage holes before filling them with soil and plants.

A few years ago most wine barrels and nail kegs were usually given away. But today these old-fashioned products are very much in demand, so they are no longer free. A sawed-in-half wine barrel can cost almost as much as a standard commercial plant container of comparable size. I recently paid $17 for a three-quarter barrel, about 30 inches in diameter, in which I planted a small fruit tree.

Butter Drums and Soy Kegs

Used sixty-pound butter drums are especially handsome, but they are hard to find. The one possible container that has yet to be "discovered," and so is still worth the cheap price, is the soy keg. Soy kegs come in 10-, 12-, and 14-inch diameters. The wood is hard and durable, and the metal bands add an attractive finish to these containers.

CHAPTER 5

Growing Vegetables Vertically—Trellises

With trellises you can grow vegetables in an area as small as 10 x 10 feet. Commercially made trellises are available in stock sizes, but they are flimsy and not very durable. It is best to construct your own trelliswork in the pattern you personally prefer. Vining vegetables such as cucumbers, peppers, tomatoes, and squash actually grow better vertically than on the ground. Other advantages are that fewer insects invade vertical gardens, and the cultivation of plants is easier. (You can also grow vegetables vertically on posts and pyramids; these structures are permanent parts of the in-ground garden.)

LATH

Trellises are built of lath. Standard lath is redwood or cedar strips $^3/_8$-inch thick by $1\ ^5/_8$ inches wide. Redwood and cedar contain decay-resistant oil, and their straight grain renders them less susceptible to warping. Heat, cold, dryness, and moisture do not affect these woods. Laths are sold in lengths of 6, 8, and 10 feet, in bundles of 50 pieces. Standard lathing is inexpensive, easy to work with, and adaptable. Use surface lath, which is practically free of imperfections. (Milled lath contains knotholes and blemishes.) Bundled lathing will last 2 to 3 years.

Free Standing Trellis

Michael Valdez

Lath can also be made of 1 x 1, 1 x 2, or 2 x 2 inch wood cut to size and sold by the running foot rather than by the bundle. Such lathing is more expensive than the bundled lath, but it is stronger and better looking. Finally, you can make your own lathing from pine or fir, but if you do, be sure to apply a protective coating of preservative or paint to protect the wood from the weather.

Lath Construction

The simplest but least sturdy method of lath construction consists of nailing and epoxying one lath upon another, in a crisscross pattern. A stronger method is to nail a 1 x 1 or 2 x 2 piece of wood to another such piece, in a crisscross or diamond pattern.

The third and strongest method is to interlock the laths, following this nine-step procedure:

Trellis and Plant Supports

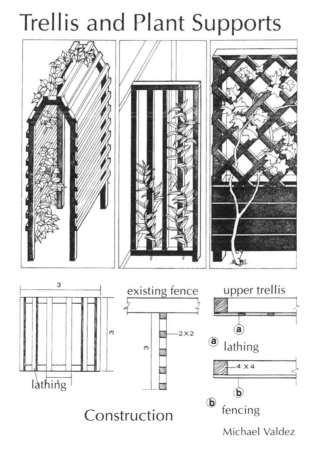

3

lathing

Construction

existing fence

2 x 2

upper trellis

(a)

(a) lathing

4 x 4

(b)

(b) fencing

Michael Valdez

1. Work with nonstandard laths: 1 x 1s or 2 x 2s.
2. Tape together bundles of 2 x 2 inch strips (10 pieces to a bundle), with the ends flush.
3. Across all the pieces, mark parallel 1- inch-wide lines; space the lines evenly.
4. On your saw, tape masking tape lengthwise to a 1-inch depth. Saw down as far as the tape, just inside your markings.
5. With a small hammer, strike between the saw cuts to knock out the chunks of wood, leaving a socket or groove.
6. Insert 1 x 1 inch wood strips crossways into the grooves (they should fit flush).
7. Make the frame from 2 x 4s.
8. Nail strips into grooved pieces.
9. Paint the lattice, or leave it natural.

Spacing Laths

50

Space laths correctly to (1) create a definite pattern, (2) give plants enough room to grasp the wood, and (3) create shadow and light patterns. Here is the recommended spacing formula: for lath $^1/_2$-inch or less thick, use $^3/_4$-inch spacing; for lath $^1/_2$- to 1-inch thick, use $^3/_4$-inch spacing; for lath 2 inches thick, use 1- to 2-inch spacing. Be sure spacing is consistent throughout the pattern, because variations will be noticeable.

Space correctly by using a spacer, a wooden block 6 to 8 inches long inserted between the laths as you nail them in place. Lay the spacer flat on top as you nail the top of the lath in place and again lay it flat near the bottom when you nail the bottom of the lath in place.

BUYING LUMBER

How much lumber you will need is determined by the total area of the trelliswork, the size of the laths you are using, and the amount of spacing you are allowing. To determine how many bundles of standard lath to buy (if that is what you are using), figure the number of running feet per bundle and divide this amount into number of running feet required. The amount of running feet per bundle is the length of the lath times the number of laths in the bundle. For example, a bundle of 50 laths, each lath 6 feet long, consists of 300 running feet: 50 x 6 = 300.

As discussed earlier, I recommend using nonstandard laths, 1 x 1, 1 x 2, or 2 x 2 inch, sold by the running foot. Use this formula to determine how much of the heavier lath to order:

1. Find the number of running feet of lath required per square foot of area: Add the width of the lath to the space you plan to leave between the lath and divide the total into 12: 1 $\frac{1}{2}$-inch lath spaced $\frac{1}{2}$-inch apart: 12÷1 $\frac{1}{2}$ + $\frac{1}{2}$ = 12÷2 = 6
2. To determine how many running feet you need, multiply the running feet per square foot by the total number of square feet in the area: For 6 running feet of lath per square foot and 50 square feet to cover, 300 running feet of lath are needed: 6 x 50 = 300.

FRAMING

Framing is what you nail the lathing to. It must be substantial; 2 x 4s are suitable. Rather than making very large or long frames, make a small one that is no longer than 4 feet. Nail the 2 x 4s together at the corners; brace each corner with an L-shaped brace. For additional support, you can run a piece of wood across the frame. If you use this extra support, be sure it blends in with the overall design of the trellis.

TRELLIS PATTERNS

There are numerous patterns to use, including arches and geometric shapes, but note that the more intricate the design, the more time involved in constructing the trellis. Whatever pattern you decide on, first sketch what you want; from the sketch you can determine how much lumber you will need.

Grid

The grid is the simplest and easiest pattern for trelliswork and adapts well outdoors, on fences, against walls, and in containers. Nail the lath at the top and bottom, horizontally and vertically, and then nail the other laths on top at each end. This open pattern allows good circulation of air and alternates

51

Trellis Patterns

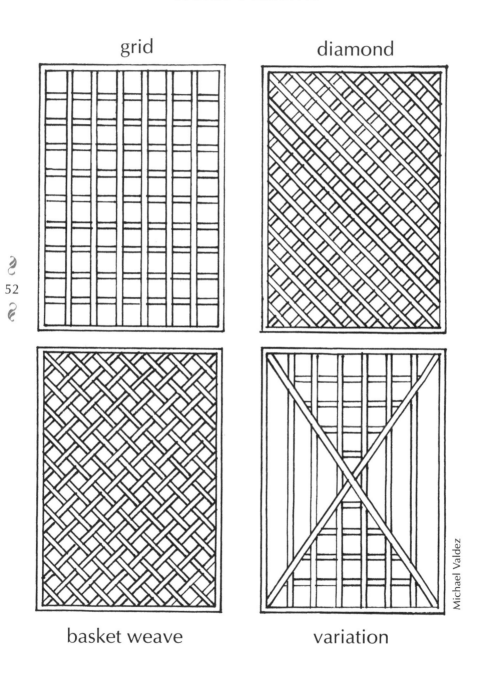

grid

diamond

basket weave

variation

52

Michael Valdez

amounts of sun and shade, which is good for vegetables. The grid spacing is usually 1 inch but can be closer.

Starburst

The starburst pattern is handsome and especially effective in entranceways and very large containers. The pattern can be horizontal or vertical.

Diamond

The diamond pattern is a variation of the grid; diamond-shaped openings rather than rectangular ones are between the lathing. This pattern is easy to make, but spacing must be absolutely consistent throughout the design. Nail laths in place at the top and bottom, left to right, and then nail the other lathing at the top and bottom, right to left. Vegetables grow well on a diamond trellis.

VEGETABLES FOR TRELLISES

Many vegetables are fine for trellis growing, but root vegetables such as carrots and beets, which grow horizontally, are grown in the standard way. Vegetables such as cabbage and cauliflower are not recommended for trellis growing. You can grow vegetables from seeds as previously mentioned or buy prestarted plants. Vegetable varieties are many, and new ones appear yearly. Varieties mentioned here are traditional ones. See catalogs for other kinds.

Beans

String beans and green beans are available in climbing and pole varieties. Plant seeds 1 inch deep, 8 inches apart when weather is settled into spring, because beans like heat. Use a rich fertile soil, and give plants plenty of water. Apply fish emulsion when pods start forming. Pick beans when they are small rather than large because their flavor is better then, and picking helps extend the harvest over many weeks. Kentucky Wonder, Blue Lake, and Ramona are good pole snap beans; they grow within 60 to 70 days. King of the Garden and Prizetaker, which grow with 90 days, are good pole lima beans.

How to Make a Trellis for Climbing Vegetables

① Select materials

② Measure vertical and horizontal posts, nail together

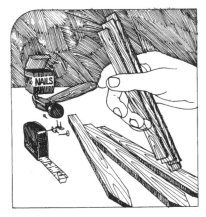

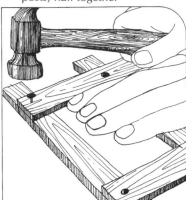

James Carew

③ Carefully secure posts into soil

④ Attach stems to trellis with string for support

Cucumbers

Cucumbers, available in dozens of varieties, look like beautiful foliage houseplants. This warm-season crop comes in smooth or warty, tiny or huge types. Plant seeds 1 inch deep and 4 inches apart. Keep moisture even at the roots, and pick the cukes as soon as they are ready, or they will not produce more harvest. Fertilize plants with rotted manure and occasionally apply fish emulsion. Burpee Hybrid, Triumph, Ashley, and Gemini Hybrid are good standard-sized cucumbers; they are ready in 60 to 65 days. Good midget varieties are Tiny Dill Cuke (ready in 55 days) and Patio Pick (ripe in 57 days).

Eggplant

Generally not considered a vegetable for vertical growing, eggplant can be trained on a trellis. Eggplant is a warm-season crop that prefers 80° Fahrenheit by day and 70° at night. Place prestarts about 4 inches apart in containers when the weather is settled (seeds take too long to germinate). Eggplant needs even moisture at its roots and good sun. Pick eggplant when it is young (about ²/₃ its mature size), and when the skin is still glossy. Do not tear off eggplant; cut it off with pruning shears. Try Black Beauty, Burpee Hybrid, and Early Beauty Hybrid, all ready in 60 to 80 days.

Peas

Peas are a great vegetable to grow because they thrive even with minimal care. A cool-season crop, peas like cool moisture in the soil; they produce in early spring and late fall (they will produce in the summer, but in lesser amounts). Plant seeds 2 inches deep, 2 inches apart; plants love to grow on trellises or poles. Give plants a lot of sun and water—never let the soil dry out. Feed peas lightly with fish emulsion, and pinch back the growing tips of stems to thin out the vine and encourage a large harvest.

Immediately harvest peas when they are mature; this keeps them producing. When left on the vine too long, peas become pithy and lose their succulent sweet taste.

Common green peas—English peas—are grown for the seed. Edible pea pods—Chinese pea pods—are grown for the pod and are called snow or sugar peas. Excellent green pea varieties are Alderman, Wando, Freezonian, and Little Marvel, all of which are ready in 60 to 75 days. Good edible pea pods are Burpee's Sweet Pod, Dwarf Gray Sugar, and Mammoth Melting Sugar, ready in 65 to 72 days.

Peppers

Peppers are warm-season plants; they are pretty plants when mature. They love temperatures above 60° Fahrenheit but not over 90°, or they will not set fruit. Plant prestarts 12 inches apart. Peppers are not naturally vining, but they do adapt to vertical growing if you tie the stems to a trellis.

Give plants lots of moisture; feed with fish emulsion when the first blooms open. Keep picking peppers as they mature to encourage more fruit, and harvest them when they are firm and crisp. You can pick them when they are green, or let them turn red on the plant. Pick hot peppers only when they are completely ripe. Sweet (bell) peppers include Burpee's Fordhook, California Wonder, Bell Boy Hybrid, and Yolo Wonder, all ready in 65 to 75 days. Long Red Cayenne, Yellow Wax Hungarian, and Large Cherry, ready in 70 days, are superb hot peppers.

Squash

Squash is so prolific, you will have more than you have ever wanted. It naturally grows horizontally, and quickly and vigorously, but it can be trained to a trellis or pole. Squash is a warm-season crop and prefers temperatures above 68° Fahrenheit.

56

Plant prestarts at the base of the trellis or pole, or plant seeds 1 inch deep, 12 inches apart. Acorn squash is the most popular of the winter squash; zucchini and golden crookneck are favorite summer squash. Harvest summer squash when they are young and tender. Winter squash can stay on the plant until they are well matured. Hubbard, Table Queen (hubbard type), and Butternut (hubbard type) are superb winter squash, ready in 85 to 110 days. Golden Summer Crookneck, Burpee's Hybrid Zucchini, and Artistocrat (zucchini) are good summer squash, ready in about 52 days.

Tomatoes

Actually a fruit, tomatoes are everyone's favorite. Even a novice gardener can be successful with this warm-season crop if the plants receive lots of sun and water. Do not plant tomatoes too early in the season. Plant seeds or prestarts deeply, so the first set of leaves is just above the soil line. Plant seeds 1/2 inch deep, 16 inches apart; place prestarts 16 inches from the base of the support.

Shake plants, or apply Blossom-Set to get tomatoes to pollinate. To set fruit, tomatoes demand nighttime temperatures between 60° and 70° Fahrenheit. Always use disease-resistant varieties (tomatoes are prone to disease). With the proper soil, tomatoes will rarely need fertilizer; in fact, too much fertilizer can produce many leaves but few fruits. Try New Yorker, Spring Giant, and Fireball—ready in 65 days—for good early season tomatoes. Better Boy, Burpee's VF Tomato, and Glamour, ready in 72 to 80 days, are recommended midseason plants. For a late-season crop, try Early Pak 7, Ace 55, Heinz 1350, and Marglobe, ready in 73 to 80 days. Red Cherry (ripe in 73 days) and Tiny Tim (ready in 55 days) are fine small tomatoes.

Chapter 6

A Bounty of Vegetables

In this chapter we describe the most popular vegetables and include what to grow them in. First, we discuss the standard-sized vegetables, and then we cover the many excellent dwarf or midget varieties. For convenience, the end of the chapter has a handy reference chart for sowing seed.

STANDARD-SIZED VEGETABLES

Beets

Beets do well in a planter. If you start seed in the fall, you should be able to keep harvesting the crop well into the winter. In early spring or early fall, scatter seed 3 to 4 inches apart; seed will germinate in 7 to 10 days. Keep the starting soil evenly moist. After germination, thin the plants to 3 inches apart. Give plants plenty of light and lots of water. Plants will mature in 55 to 60 days; pull beets when they are small (large beets will taste woody).

Beets

Michael Valdez

Carrots

Carrots can be grown in a planter, or several in a pot. In early spring, plant seeds 1 to 2 inches apart. After seed germinates in 10 to 17 days, thin plants to 2 inches apart. Carrots like bright light and an evenly moist soil; never let the soil dry out. Plants mature in 65 to 75 days; harvest carrots before they become too large or they will taste woody.

Cucumbers

Cucumbers thrive in a planter or 5-gallon tub. In the summer, plant two or three prestarts; they will germinate in 7 to 14 days. It is not necessary to thin them. Grow plants with trellis support; keep the soil evenly moist, be sure plants get warmth and sun, and feed them with a manure solution. Prestarts mature in 60 to 70 days; pick the cukes before they turn yellow (remember, the more you pick, the more you will get).

Michael Valdez

Cucumbers

59

Eggplant

Eggplant does well in a planter, or one per 10-inch pot. In March or April, sow seeds 2 to 4 inches apart. After 7 to 14 days, when seed has germinated, thin plants to 12 inches apart. When the plants reach 4 to 6 inches in height, repot them in large 24-inch tubs, 2 plants per tub. Give plants heat and plenty of water; never let the soil dry out, and be sure to feed plants. In 60 to 85 days eggplant will mature. Pick the fruit when they are about 8 inches long and shiny black.

Green Peppers

There are both sweet and hot peppers. The sweet ones are good for many dishes, but most people find the hot peppers too spicy. In late spring, plant two prestarts to a 16-inch tub. Plants will germinate in 10 to 20 days; they do not need thinning. Peppers need warmth, about 80° Fahrenheit. If they are subjected to temperatures below 60° or above 90°, they will not set fruit. Fertilize plants often, and keep the soil uniformly moist. When plants mature, in 70 to 80 days, pick the fruit when it is turning from green to red. If you leave overripe peppers on the vine, yield will be inhibited.

Lettuce

Lettuce comes in a variety of types, including leaf, romaine, butterhead, and bibb. All types are excellent. In early spring or early fall, place seed in 12- to 16-inch-diameter tubs. Plants will germinate in 4 to 20 days; no thinning is necessary. Lettuce is a cool-season vegetable and does not like heat, so grow plants some-what cool and keep the soil evenly moist. When plants mature—40 to 50 days for loose-leaf types, 65 to 85 days for butterheads, and 80 to 85 days for head lettuce—pick outer leaves as plants keep maturing. Try the varieties: Great Lakes, Penlake, and Os-wego (head type); Butter King, Buttercrunch, Summer Bibb, and Big Boston (butterheads); Oakleaf, Salad Bowl, and Prizehead (loose-leaf); Paris Island Cos and Dark Green Cos (romaine).

Radishes

Radishes require almost no care. This cool-season crop can be started at any time. Plant seeds in a planter or pot; plants germinate in 3 to 7 days, but thinning is not necessary. Give plants bright light (sun is not needed), and keep the soil evenly moist, never letting it dry out. Radishes mature in 20 to 30 days; harvest them when they are about the size of a quarter. Winter radishes can be planted in late fall.

Spinach

Spinach grows quickly. In early spring or early fall, sow seeds 2 to 4 inches apart in a 12-inch tub. When plants germinate in 6 to 14 days, thin them to 6 to 8 inches apart. Keep tubs in bright but not sunny spots (spinach will not tolerate warm temperatures). Keep soil evenly moist, not soggy, and feed plants occasionally. When plants mature in 40 to 50 days, cut off the outer leaves as you need them. Once plants set seed, they are no good.

Squash

Squash comes in summer varieties (yellow squash) and winter types (acorn squash); zucchini is for year-round growing. In the spring, plant two prestarts to a 5-inch tub; they will germinate in 5 to 12 days. No thinning is necessary. Give plants warmth, additional feeding, tons of water, and a sunny location. Summer squash matures in 50 to 55 days, winter squash in 85 days. Harvest squash while it is still small, about 4 to 8 inches long.

Tomatoes

Tomatoes are the most popular fruit grown. Besides the standard types, midget (cocktail or cherry) tomatoes are also delicious (see the section on dwarf vegetables in this chapter). These plants must be staked to a trellis or a support, or they become a mess if they grow naturally with nowhere to climb. In spring or late summer, sow seeds 2 to 3 inches apart. Plants germinate in 6 to 14 days, at which time you should thin them to 10 inches apart. Tomatoes must have tons of water and warmth, above 60° Fahrenheit, or they will not produce fruit. Soil must be kept evenly moist or blossom end rot may infect plants. Plants also need additional feeding. Seedlings mature in about 50 days (prestarts will mature in less time). Pick tomatoes when they are turning red.

61

DWARF VEGETABLES

Midget vegetables are perfect for containers. All kinds of vegetables can be grown, from beets to tomatoes. The dwarfs can be grown from seed or from prestarts that are sold in season at nurseries. The dwarfs are as easy to grow as the standard vegetables, perhaps even easier because you will have less "plant" to contend with. If you are growing vegetables in a small area or want to do just container gardening, dwarfs are the perfect solution, and rest assured that no taste will be sacrificed.

Beets

The one true midget beet in my experience is Spinel, which takes 50 to 60 days to mature to its 1-inch-wide size. The Ruby Queen, however, can also fit into a garden of dwarfs; it matures in 56 days.

Make the first planting in early spring, a month before the last frost. Make other plantings every 3 weeks until early summer for a continuous crop; plant again in late summer.

Plant seeds ¹/₂-inch deep, Spinel seeds 1 ¹/₂ inches, Ruby Queen seed 4 inches apart. Be sure to keep the seeds moist, and thin them after they germinate.

Carrots

The appeal of dwarf carrots is their special delicate flavor, sometimes a definite sweetness. Begin carrots a month before the last spring frost; they can be seeded every 3 weeks until early summer. Plant seed ¹/₂-inch deep; thin seedlings to 2 inches apart (Short 'N Sweet, Red Apple, Gourmet Parisienne, Gold Nugget), 1 inch apart for other midgets. Give carrots partial shade.

Red Apple is 1 ¹/₂ inches long and wide and sweet. It matures in 65 days, as do Gourmet Parisienne and Gold Nugget. Sucram matures in 50 to 70 days; it is ³/₄-inch wide and 5 inches long. Baby-Finger Nantes is quite tender; it matures in 50 days. It tastes best at harvest when the vegetables are barely mature.

Sugarstick and Midget mature in 65 days. Little Finger is virtually coreless and about 4 inches long, Tiny Sweet is 3 inches long and matures in 65 days.

Cucumbers

Midget cucumbers have pretty heart-shaped foliage. Growth habit is vining or bushy; no plants grow taller than 36 inches, with cucumbers 3 to 4 inches long. Water plants heavily because they must have ample moisture. Feed twice during the growing season. Plants will mature in 55 days. Tiny Dill and Little Minnie are fine varieties; hybrids Patio Pik and Cherokee are disease-resistant.

Eggplant

The small Japanese eggplant, about 5 inches long, is what started me growing this vegetable, after which I went on to Morden Midget, which matures in about 65 days. Give plants summer heat and lots of sun, a very rich soil, plenty of moisture, and feeding. Harvest plants as soon as the food shows good color.

Green Peppers

Peppers are handsome plants with attractive foliage and fruit; they add welcome color to any garden. Grow pepper plants in hot weather and give them plenty of water. Feeding is not necessary. Peppers ripen their fruit in slow succession, so you have a harvest for many weeks. Pinocchio and Tokyo Bell both mature in 60 days.

Okra

Okra produces pretty hibiscuslike flowers; this vegetable tastes good when cooked with onions and tomatoes. Okra does not need a very rich soil; give plants plenty of water and heat. When plants mature, in 50 to 60 days, keep pods picked.

Peas

Peas make for wonderful eating. In early spring, sow seeds 2 inches apart. Seed will germinate in 6 to 15 days; after germination, thin plants to 6 to 8 inches apart. Give plants brightness (not sun), even moisture, and some additional feeding. They will mature in 50 to 60 days. Start picking the peas when the pods have swelled to a round shape; pick every few days (do not let them stay on the vine too long). Pinch back growing tips to encourage yield. Good varieties are Mighty Midget, Tiny Tim, and Dwarf Gray Sugar.

63

Tomatoes

Tomatoes are the most popular of the dwarfs. Grow prestarts, and water them copiously. Feed them with a 10-20-10 plant food or a special tomato food. Harvest plants at 55 days. Tiny Tim grows only 16 inches tall; Patio Hybrid reaches 28 inches.

TABLE—VEGETABLE SEED INFORMATION (OUTDOORS)

Vegetable	Distance Between Plants (inches)	Distance Between Rows (inches)	Plant Seed Depth (inches)	Germination Temperature (0° Fahrenheit)	Germination Time (days)
Beans:					
Garden	6–8	18–20	1 1/2–2	68–86	5–8
Lima	6–8	24–30	1 1/2–2	68–86	5–9
Runner	6–8	Grow vertically	1 1/2–2	68–86	5–9
Beet	2	12–14	1	68–86	3–14
Broccoli	12–14	24–30	1/2	68–86	3–10
Cabbage	16–20	24–30	1/2	68–86	3–10
Cabbage, Chinese	12–18	20–24	1/2	68–86	3–7
Carrot	1–2	12–18	1/4	68–86	6–21
Cauliflower	8–10	30–34	1/2	68–86	3–10
Cress, garden	10–12	12–16	1/4	68	4–7
Cucumber	10	40–50	1	68–86	4–10
Eggplant	12–16	30–36	1/2	68–86	7–14
Escarole (endive)	9–12	12–24	1/2	68–86	5–14
Leek	2–4	12–18	1/2–1	68	6–14
Lettuce	12–14	18–20	1/4–1/2	68	7
Okra	15–18	28–30	1	68–86	4–14
Onion	2–3	12–14	1/2	68	6–10
Pea	2–3	Grow vertically	2	68	5–8
Pepper	16–18	24–30	1/4	68–86	6–14
Radish	1–2	6–12	1/2	68	4–5
Spinach	2–4	12–14	1/2	59	7–21
Squash	20–24	Grow vertically	1	68–86	4–7
Tomato	18–30	30–48	1/2	68–86	5–14

CHAPTER 7

Harvesting and Storing the Bounty

The joy of vegetable gardening is that not only do you get wonderfully tasty produce for your table, but you get such an abundant crop that you can give food away to friends and still have enough to store for future meals. Vegetables are especially welcome in the winter months, when stores usually have the minimum amount of fresh produce. By storing your bounty, you can enjoy tomatoes, squash, and other vegetables year-round, keeping your taste buds happy and your body healthy.

HARVESTING TIPS

Whether you plan on eating your vegetables immediately or saving them for later eating pleasure, you should know when to pluck them from the plant. Tomatoes should be almost red; carrots should be yellow and picked right away; they will become tough if left in the soil too long.

Cucumbers keep multiplying even after you pick them, when they are firm and nicely green. Pick eggplants at maturity, when they have reached full size. Pick peas and sweet peppers when their size is right; keep plucking lettuce leaves as needed.

STORAGE METHODS

The four methods of storing vegetables are common storage, drying, canning, and freezing. Common storage is keeping root vegetables in cool, unheated, and dark places such as pantries, garages, and cupboards. Drying retains all vitamins except for vitamin C. Canning involves using pressure or a bath of boiling water. Freezing is a simple method that retains high amounts of nutrients, but some vegetables, such as cucumbers and lettuce, cannot be frozen.

Common Storage

Root cellars, outdoor pits, barrels or boxes in the garage, and cellars are great places for storing vegetables. A root cellar, which has a dirt floor and is not heated, should be cool but not freezing. If you use barrels or boxes, bury the vegetables in sand in the containers. Common storage is fine for carrots, beets, turnips, and squash. Follow these recommendations for successful storage:

66

1. Handle vegetables carefully to avoid bruising them.
2. Before storing root vegetables, let them cool a few hours after you harvest them to dissipate the field heat.
3. Dry vegetables before storing them (a few hours to overnight is fine).
4. Keep storage temperature at 35° to 55° Fahrenheit, depending on what you are storing (see p. 67).
5. Be sure ventilation is good and humidity is high in the storage area.
6. Leave some stems on vegetables when storing them.
7. Leave space between vegetables in storage.
8. Keep the storage area clean.

I have never washed my vegetables before storing them, and I have had no problems. It is more important that the vegetables are thoroughly dry. Dry sand or sawdust are good packing materials.

A good outdoor storage area is a cone-shaped mound in a well-drained location. Put a layer of straw or leaves on the ground, with a layer of hardware cloth on top (to keep out rodents). Stack the vegetables in layers on the cloth, cover the pile with more leaves or straw, and put 3 to 4 inches of soil over the pile. Continue to put more straw and leaves over the soil, with boards over the soil to keep rain away. Ventilate the mound by inserting three stakes through the center (to form a flue); cap the flue with hardware cloth.

Vegetable	Storage Site	Temperature (0° Fahrenheit)	Humidity	Storage Time
Cabbage	pit	32	moist	fall/winter
Carrots and beets	pit, cellar	32	moist	fall/winter
Peppers	unheated room	45–50	moist	3–4 weeks
Squash	cellar	55	dry	fall/winter
Tomatoes (green)	cellar	55	dry	4–6 weeks

Drying

Root vegetables adapt very well to drying, and removing moisture from food reduces the possibility of any bacteria or fungi (which decompose food) from growing. Pick vegetables when they are ripe, and dry them within a few hours. With a stainless steel knife (to prevent discoloration), cut the vegetables into uniform slices or pieces. You should precook (blanch) all vegetables but onions to inhibit the growing of enzymes with the food. To blanch, plunge the cut vegetables into boiling water and leave in the water 5 to 20 minutes. Next, place the vegetables into cold water for 1 minute and then carefully dry them.

Dry your vegetables in the oven. You should use wood-framed trays covered with coarse cloth. Preheat gas ovens to 150° Fahrenheit and leave the door open. Move the trays to different levels so the vegetables dry evenly—top tray to the bottom, then to the middle, and so on. Set electric ovens at 200° Fahrenheit for 2 to 3 hours, and then lower the temperature to 150° Fahrenheit. Leave the door slightly open. It will take about 10 hours for your vegetables to dry. The more you turn the food while it is drying, the better it will be because it will receive an even distribution of heat. Cut the vegetables at their thickest parts; if the texture and appearance are uniform throughout, the food is correctly dried. After the vegetables have dried, immediately store them in airtight containers in a cool, dry place. This will ensure no insect infestation. You can also buy commercial drying units from grower's catalogs.

Here is quick reference chart for oven-drying vegetables:

Vegetable	Preparation	Cooking Time (Minutes)	Oven Temperature
Beets	wash	until done	150°
Cabbage	trim	12	140°
Carrots	wash, scrub	8–12	160°
Onions	skin	5–7	130°
Peas	shell, wash	3	140°
Squash	wash, stem, cut open, seed, peel	15	150°

Freezing

Freezing is the easiest storage method. Pick vegetables at the peak of their maturity and freeze them immediately; this will ensure the greatest freshness. After picking the vegetables, wash them thoroughly in cold water (wash only 2 pounds at a time). Then place them in a wire basket or a cheesecloth bag.

Blanch the vegetables (cook them briefly in boiling water or steam) in a large covered kettle in 1 gallon of rapidly boiling water. Immerse the basket or bag in the water for 3 to 5 minutes; remove and immediately chill the vegetables by plunging them into a kettle of icy water or holding them under cold running water.

Beans, beets, broccoli, carrots, peas, squash, and peppers (do not blanch peppers) freeze well, but not tomatoes. With greens such as spinach, blanch for only 1 or 2 minutes.

Packaging

Properly packaging vegetables is the secret to successful freezing. Plastic bags, heavy-duty aluminum foil, and freezer paper work fine if they are airtight. If you use plastic bags, be sure to press out as much air as possible before sealing the bags. The heat-and-seal bag is a wonderful invention that allows you to freeze the vegetables in the bag and then reheat them in the same bag.

Try to freeze vegetables in flat packages for easy stacking. Keep the freezer temperature at 0° Fahrenheit. Mark the contents and date on the packages.

CHAPTER 8

Sprouts and Herbs

When my garden helper arrived at my door a few years ago with a bag of sprouts as his lunch, I naturally scoffed. But I tasted—hesitantly—then chewed with enthusiasm. The sprouts were fresh-tasting, crisp alfalfa shoots the boy had started in a mayonnaise jar. Because I'm a garden-green enthusiast, I quizzed him about his growing techniques; this in turn produced an hour-long lecture from him on the virtue of sprouts. I suppose I could repeat his lecture here in full, but will spare you instead. Put simply, sprouts have exceptional nutrient content. Growing alfalfa sprouts and munching them didn't change my life or make me an overnight champion— but the sprouts did furnish me with some very good eating, and soon I was growing all kinds. And so were other people! By the time I had had my fill of sprouts, tons of sprouting gadgets had appeared on the market.

Sprouts can be grown anyplace in your home; they don't need sunlight to grow. Sprouts herald spring and put some spring in you, too. More importantly, in salads or soups or just nibbles during the day, sprouts are both a refreshing treat and a tonic. Sprouting isn't only a good way to provide more natural vitamins and minerals for you and your family, it's also easy to do and cheap. But what to sprout? For a starter, try alfalfa, mung beans, lentils, and soybeans. (Local health and organic food stores carry these seeds.) Alfalfa sprouts, sometimes called the king of sprouts, are rich in potassium, phosphorus, calcium, sodium, magnesium, and chlorophyll. Eating alfalfa also is considered good for skin conditions, and some say alfalfa helps to soothe aching arthritic conditions. Actually, alfalfa isn't a wonder food, but alfalfa sprouts and other kinds can add new zest to your health and to your cooking.

SPROUTS FROM SEEDS

Sprouts are grown from untreated seeds. Seeds themselves are storehouses containing proteins, carbohydrates, and fat—food for the plant, and for you too. What you're eating is actually the very beginning of the plant at the first few sprouts.

As mentioned, buy seeds for sprouting at health-food stores; they stock variable grain and legumes for sprouting. (Many packaged seeds sold at nurseries have been treated with insecticide mixtures and other compounds to keep them viable, so remember that only untreated seeds should be used for sprouts.) Always try to get fresh seeds without cracks or bruises; most seeds are sold in bulk or packaged in plastic or boxes.

If you don't use seeds immediately, store them in a dry, cool place. Use glass jars with lids, and label the jars so you won't forget what they hold. Seeds and sprouts assume many different shapes, so it's wise to keep track of what you grow.

Be sure to cut your sprouts before they become plants; harvest most sprouts when they're $1/2$ to 2 inches long. If you aren't going to eat your sprouts right away, store them; rinse them well, and drain them for a few hours after the final rinse before storage. Sprouts store better if there's no excess moisture clinging to them. Store them in plastic jars or plastic containers; don't use plastic bags because humidity may accumulate and ruin the sprouts, or they may get crushed. Most sprouts will last about a week under refrigeration before spoiling.

Alfalfa

Alfalfa is widely used in many countries as forage for animals. Sprouted seeds are rich in vitamins D, E, and K. They also have vital cell-building amino acids and as a bonus contain phosphorus, calcium, sodium, potassium, and other nutrients of value to the body. The seeds are about 35 percent protein, and the sprouts are fresh, crispy, and flavorful. Use alfalfa sprouts in sandwiches, soups, and salads for a tasty variation in your diet.

Beans

There's a large variety of beans good for sprouting: fava, lima, and so forth. Beans have been an inexpensive common food in many countries, highly prized for their nutrient value. Beans and other legumes are the richest source of protein you can buy and are also an excellent source of iron and niacin. Most beans are easily sprouted and can be used in many ways in soups and salads. Each variety of bean sprout has its own distinct, succulent flavor, and when cooked with vegetables they are delicious.

Chickpeas

Chickpeas are 20 percent protein and have some iron and good quantities of vitamins A and C. They're easy to sprout, and they can be used effectively in soups, salads, and other foods. The lowly chickpea is high on the list of good sprouts.

Garden Cress

Garden cress is somewhat difficult to sprout because temperatures must be kept in the cool range (never higher than 68° Fahrenheit). The plant is used best in winter salads and coleslaws and has a wonderful peppery taste. Cress has large quantities of vitamins A and C; use garden cress fresh, not cooked.

Lentils

Lentils are an underrated but absolutely delicious annual herb. Small lentils (usually sold in plastic packages) are more flavorful than large ones. Lentils have ample amounts of protein, iron, and phosphorus. The sprouts may be eaten raw or cooked—an excellent source of nourishment.

Mung Beans

These beans deserve a special section of their own because they're so popular; they're grown in great quantities in the Orient because bean sprouts are a favorite part of Chinese cooking. Mung beans, an annual herb, have a good supply of vitamin E and are simply delicious. Use them in cooked dishes such as casseroles, or try them fresh in salads.

Peas

Peas are almost 20 percent protein and contain essential amino acids; they are an annual vine, and the sprouts have a lovely fresh green flavor similar to fresh peas. Peas sprout easily and can be used in soups and salads.

Pumpkin Seeds

These sprouts are more nutritious than you might think: They contain large amounts of iron and are 30 percent protein (years ago they were used as folk medicine). Use hulled seeds, and eat sprouted seeds raw or slightly toasted. Pumpkin-seed sprouts also can be used in salads and soups.

73

Soybeans

Used in Oriental cookery for centuries, soybeans are now becoming popular in the United States. Recently you might have noticed that soybeans are used in hamburger to boost the protein factor—soybeans are 30 percent protein. They also contain lecithin, which supposedly helps to reduce cholesterol. Soybeans are sometimes hard to sprout and need frequent rinsing throughout the day.

STARTING SPROUTS

Directions are provided with the commercial sprouting devices previously mentioned, so I don't have to say more about them. Sprouts start easily, so use the inexpensive methods: jars, flowerpots, cans, or trays. Each method is delightfully simple—just make your choice.

Mayonnaise Jars

Wash a mayonnaise jar thoroughly and dry it. Stuff a handful of sphagnum moss (sold at nurseries) inside the jar; add 2 ounces of alfalfa, beans, or other seeds, and enough water to thoroughly moisten the sphagnum. Stretch a piece of cheesecloth over the mouth of the jar and secure it with a sturdy rubber band or a mason jar ring cap; now tilt the jar to drain the excess water through the mesh. Keep the sphagnum evenly moist, but never wet, and rinse seeds daily. You'll be harvesting sprouts in a few days.

Flowerpots

Growing sprouts in flowerpots is slightly more sophisticated than growing them in mayonnaise jars. Use an 8-inch clay pot with drainage holes. Place a piece of burlap at the bottom of the pot, and put a stone over the burlap. Add 2 ounces of mung beans, and weigh down another swatch of burlap over the beans. Water the beans, letting the water drain out. Then cover the pot with a plastic food bag to ensure good humidity. Rinse the sprouts a few times a day. Put the pot in a bright, but not sunny, place.

Cans

Cut out the top and bottom of a can. Slip a plastic cottage-cheese carton or similar container into the can. (Be sure to punch drain holes in the plastic carton.) Add lentils, soybeans, or mung beans. Put a small bit of burlap with a stone. Water the beans, let the water drain, and cover the can with a plastic food bag. Rinse as directed in the table "Sprouting at a Glance" on p. 75. Lay a close mesh-wire screen on the bottom of a wooden tray, and set your beans on the screen. Cover the tray with cheesecloth and water the beans. Now cover the container with a plastic food bag.

Helpful Hints

Here are some useful rules for growing sprouts of all kinds:

- To be sure there's sufficient air underneath containers that drain from the bottom, set them on wood blocks or bricks.

74

- Never leave seeds in water for more than 10 hours without rinsing.
- Use tepid water for sprouting.
- Don't sprout seeds for longer than 4 days, or your sprouts will become plants.
- Never let seeds or sprouts dry out. Rinse them at least twice a day, sometimes 3 to 4 times a day.
- Don't buy treated seeds, because they may contain pesticides.
- Don't put sprouts in direct sunlight; average bright light is best.

Sprouting at a Glance

Type of fresh, untreated seeds for sprouts
Normal germination time
Recommended temperature (in ° Fahrenheit)
Recommended daily rinse frequently
Recommended harvesting length (in inches)
Proportional yields (Seeds: Sprouts)

75

RECIPES

Sprouts

Alfalfa Sprout Muffins

2 cups Bisquick
2 teaspoons baking powder
$^1/_2$ teaspoon salt
1 egg, beaten
2 tablespoons honey
1 cup half-and-half
$^1/_4$ cup softened margarine
1 cup alfalfa sprouts, finely cut

Combine Bisquick, baking powder, and salt. In a separate bowl, mix together egg, honey, cream, and margarine. Add alfalfa sprouts to the liquids, and pour mixture into the dry ingredients. Mix only slightly. Spoon mixture onto a greased baking pan to form 2-inch biscuits. Bake at 400° Fahrenheit for 15 minutes. Makes approximately 24 muffins.

Crunchy Salad

1 large tomato, sliced
1 cup alfalfa sprouts
2 cups lettuce, chopped head
2 tablespoons lemon juice
3 tablespoons salad oil
salt and pepper to taste

Mix together tomato slices and half of the sprouts in a bowl, then add sections of crisp lettuce. Pour lemon juice and oil mixture over salad. Add remaining sprouts. Toss lightly, coating ingredients with dressing, and season with salt and pepper. Serves 4.

Alfalfa Sprout Omelet

3 egg yolks
$^1/_2$ teaspoon salt
$^1/_4$ cup cheddar cheese, grated
3 egg whites
1 cup alfalfa sprouts
1 tablespoon mayonnaise
1 $^1/_2$ tablespoons margarine

Beat together egg yolks, salt, and cheese. Fold in egg whites and alfalfa sprouts. Blend in mayonnaise. Melt margarine in frying pan. Pour egg mixture into pan, and cook it slowly over low heat until almost firm. Fold omelet over gently and cook another minute or two. Serves 2.

Stuffed Tomatoes

3 large tomatoes
3 hard-boiled eggs, finely chopped
$^1/_2$ cup mayonnaise
1 tablespoon minced shallots
$^1/_2$ cup alfalfa sprouts
garnish: watercress

Scoop out centers of tomatoes and dispose of pulp. Mix eggs with mayonnaise, shallots, and sprouts. Place mixture into hollowed-out tomato shells. Garnish with watercress. Serves 3.

Tomato Sprout Soup

3 whole tomatoes
2 cups milk
1 cup chopped alfalfa sprouts
Garnish: croutons

Chop tomatoes into 1-inch cubes and simmer for a few minutes. Add alfalfa sprouts and milk. Simmer briefly and turn off heat. Serve with croutons on top. Serves 4 to 6.

Lentils

Lentils have been grown by many cultures and are native to central Asia. They are annual herbs and are either brown or red in color and small in size. There is also a yellow lentil but it's rather inferior to others in flavor. Lentils are about 25 percent protein and also have good amounts of vitamin B, iron, and phosphorus. Lentil sprouts may be eaten raw in salads or steamed and served with butter or spices. Generally, lentils sprout easily and are an excellent addition to your family menus.

77

Lentil Soup

2 tablespoons margarine
1 onion, finely minced
1 carrot, thinly sliced
2 large tomatoes, chopped
1 stalk celery, chopped
4 cups lentil sprouts
3 cups vegetable or beef stock
1 1/2 teaspoons salt
1/4 teaspoon ground black pepper

Heat margarine in pan and add onion; sauté for 5 minutes over low heat. Add carrot, tomatoes, celery, lentil sprouts, and stock. Cover and cook over low heat 20 minutes. Add salt and pepper. Serves 6 to 8.

Cooked Lentils and Greens

2 cups lentil sprouts
2 tablespoons margarine

1 tomato, chopped
1 bunch spinach, chopped
1 tablespoon parsley, chopped
$^1/_2$ teaspoon salt
garnish: lemon wedges

Sauté sprouts in margarine until limp. Add tomato and other measured ingredients. Cover and cook about 7 minutes. Garnish with lemon wedges. Serves 4 to 6.

Lentil Sprout Beef Stew

2 tablespoons olive oil
2 pounds stew meat, cubed
1 cup water
2 carrots, sliced
3 potatoes, quartered
1 green pepper, chopped
1 tomato, chopped
1 teaspoon salt
2 cups lentil sprouts
1 cup beef broth

Heat oil in casserole dish and braise meat. Add water; cover and cook until meat is tender. Add remaining ingredients and simmer covered for 1 hour in oven at 250° Fahrenheit. Serves 6 to 8.

Mung Beans

Mung beans are probably the oldest known bean for eating and sprouting. Like most sprouts, mung beans taste best eaten raw, when they're crisp and solid. Harvest these sprouts when they're 2 inches long; you can store them for a few days in a refrigerator, but once they get brown they must be discarded. Be sure to sprout mung beans in a dark place. Here are some good mung bean recipes.

Green Salad with Mung Beans

1 head lettuce, shredded
1 tomato, sliced
salad dressing
2 cups sprouted mung beans

First toss greens and tomatoes with oil and vinegar or your favorite dressing; add mung sprouts at the last moment. Serves 4 to 6.

Scrambled Eggs and Sprouts

Make your usual scrambled egg recipe, add $^1/_4$ cup of chopped mung bean sprouts (per serving) when the eggs are almost set.

Sukiyaki

1 teaspoon cooking oil
1 pound beef round or sirloin, thinly sliced
$^3/_4$ cup soy sauce
$^1/_2$ cup brown sugar
2 carrots, chopped
1 bunch green onions, chopped
2 cups mung bean sprouts

Put thin coating of oil in skillet and heat to high temperature, then add meat and stir a few seconds to brown. Add soy sauce and sugar, and bring to a boil. Add carrots and onions; cook for 3 minutes. Add mung bean sprouts and remove skillet from heat. Let stand a few seconds and serve. Serves 4 to 6.

Mung Bean Salad

3 cups cabbage, shredded
$^1/_4$ cup pineapple, crushed
1 cup mung bean sprouts
$^1/_2$ cup mayonnaise
salt and pepper to taste
garnish: paprika

Lightly mix measured ingredients together in a large bowl. Add salt and pepper; top with paprika. Serves 4.

Egg Foo Young

1 tablespoon cooking oil
1 green pepper, finely chopped
3 eggs, slightly beaten

1 shallot, finely chopped
¹/₂ teaspoon salt
2 cups mung bean sprouts

Coat griddle with oil and turn heat on high. Mix all ingredients well in a bowl, then spoon the mixture onto the griddle. Sauté lightly on both sides until browned. Serve immediately. Serves 2.

Sprout Chop Suey

¹/₂ cup cooking oil
1 green pepper, cubed
¹/₂ cup celery, cubed
2 green onions, finely minced
1 cup boiling water
2 tablespoons soy sauce
2 tablespoons cornstarch
2 cups mung bean sprouts
1 teaspoon salt
ground black pepper to taste
¹/₂ cup sliced water chestnuts
¹/₂ cup diced bamboo shoots

Heat oil in skillet over medium heat; sauté green pepper, celery, and green onions for 4 minutes. Add boiling water, then cover and cook an additional 10 minutes. Drain the water into a mixing bowl and add the soy sauce and cornstarch to make a paste. Add the mung bean sprouts, salt, and ground pepper to the cooked vegetables and mix. Add the paste mixture, stirring constantly until sauce thickens. Mix in the water chestnuts and bamboo shoots, and serve over hot rice. Serves 4 to 6.

Soybeans

The soybean is a close relative of the mung bean but is somewhat harder to sprout. However, soybeans are worth the effort because they're particularly high in vitamin C; ¹/₂ cup of soybeans is equivalent to six glasses of orange juice. Soybeans also contain vitamin B and are an excellent source of minerals.

To be sure you sprout soybeans successfully, change the water at least three or four times while soaking them during their 12-hour swelling period.

HERBS

To me, herbs are an essential part of good cooking and excellent to drink in teas. Herbs contribute to good health via homemade medicinal compounds, and they have delightful fragrances.

Unfortunately, store-bought herbs are pretty expensive; buying about twenty different seasonings can cost you a small fortune. Also, store-bought herbs are relatively bland. They seem to lose a great deal of fragrance and flavoring when processed, packaged, and stored, so why not grow your own?

Many herbs adapt well to indoor quarters. And all kinds of herb seeds, from basil to thyme, are sold by suppliers. You can also buy young plants. Your indoor herbs won't be as luxurious as those you grow outside—indoors, growth will be slower, and plants will be smaller—but you'll still have a fine harvest as well as lovely foliage or flowering plants. Read the following pages for almost all you ever wanted to know about herbs and what they're used for.

Herbs and Their Uses

Cooking, Salads	Teas	Fragrances
Chervil	Bergamot	Marjoram
Chives	Catnip	Rosemary
Dill	Chamomile	Thyme
Marjoram	Costmary	
Oregano	Feverfew	
Parsley	Lemon balm	
Rosemary	Lovage	
Sage	Mint (many kinds)	
Summer savory	Pennyroyal	
Sweet basil	Sweet marjoram	
Tarragon	Sweet woodruff	
Thyme	Thyme	
Winter savory	Verbena	
	Yarrow	

Growing herbs is almost like growing house plants, but there's a little variation involved: The preparation of the soil and pots, the watering needed, the required temperature—in other words, general growing conditions—are all somewhat different. I prefer to grow herbs in 10-inch clay pots, but you can grow several herbs in a long wooden planter on a kitchen windowsill. In fact, practically any container 6 to 8 inches deep is all right, as long as it has enough drainage holes—herbs can't tolerate excess water at the roots.

Use any packaged soil, but add 1/2 cup or more of rotted manure (sold in sacks) and perhaps a handful of gardener's sand. Start herbs from seeds, or use "prestarts." Once herbs are growing, be sure they have at least 4 hours of sun a day, and keep the soil evenly moist—never soggy or excessively dry.

So far it all seems easy, but here's where herbs deviate from house plants: Herbs like cool temperatures. This means your herbs should be growing in a spot that's between 60° and 70° Fahrenheit during the day and between 50° and 60° Fahrenheit at night. In Chicago I grew my herbs in an unheated pantry that had a south window, and they flourished. But if you don't have an unheated pantry, try the coolest part of the kitchen, or another room.

Besides the right container, soil, and temperature, herbs need pinching and trimming more than house plants do. Don't butcher your herbs; keep them in bounds by carefully pruning errant stems and removing any decayed or brown growth. You can't miss if you remember that pruning herbs involves simply cutting a few inches off growing tips.

Herbs are either annual or perennial; annual herbs live only one season, whereas perennials grow, become dormant, and come up again the next year. Most culinary herbs—basil, chives, marjoram, parsley, rosemary, sage—can be harvested at any time during the growing season. Pick the cooking herbs fresh: green, fresh-looking leaves, not yellow or withered ones. Don't take too many leaves from a plant. However, if the plants are mature and large, you can take off their growing tips; cut about 3 to 4 inches from the plants. This cutting will encourage branching.

Homegrown herbs are used fresh, but you can pick and dry them for later use. Harvest herbs for drying when the flowers start to open. Annual herbs can sometimes be harvested in early summer; then they'll produce a new crop by fall. Perennials should be cut back yearly, after flowering, to encourage new growth.

Drying herbs for future use is simple: Just pick them and expose them to warm, dry air. The air must circulate around the herbs to absorb the moisture. Sunlight may damage leaves and the herb's flavor, so keep herbs out of the sun when they are drying. Dry herbs by tying them in bunches and hanging the bunches upside down in a warm, dry room. When the herbs are dry and crackly, take them down and carefully remove the leaves. Store the herbs in airtight containers (remember to label each container).

You can also dry herbs in screen trays. These wooden boxes (sometimes called drying boxes) have screen surfaces that facilitate evaporation. Place the picked herb leaves on the screen, leaving space between the leaves so air can circulate. Every few days stir or turn the leaves so they dry evenly and thoroughly. When the leaves are crisp and thoroughly dry, remove them from the drying screens and store them in labeled, airtight containers.

So far we've talked about herbs mostly as useful plants—for cooking, fragrance, and so forth—but herbs are also decorative plants. As such, they can add much beauty indoors on windowsills in any room. Small herb gardens are pleasing to the eye, especially when grown in groups.

You might want to try a dish-garden grouping—that is, several herbs arranged in special containers, sometimes called bonsai dishes. These containers, perhaps 12 inches wide by 6 inches long, are sold at nurseries and come in attractive colors. Grow the plants as described: with good light, even moisture, and in packaged soil. Some of the most attractive decorative herbs are noted below:

- *Spearmint.* Broad, crinkly green leaves.
- *Sage (Salvia* spp). Many colorfully leaved varieties.
- *Thyme.* Small plants that grow to 10 inches, with oval gray-green leaves.

- *Rosemary.* An excellent cascading plant with narrow, needlelike leaves.
- *Geraniums.* Rose geranium *(Pelargonium graveolens)* has handsome leaves, and lemon-scented geranium *(P. crispum)* has tiny, crinkly green leaves. Apple-scented geranium *(P. odoratissimum)* has lovely ruffled leaves.

There are many kinds of herbs, but the following ones seem to grow best indoors.

Basil

This is an attractive annual herb. The most popular basil is sweet basil, which has shiny green leaves and small white flowers. Basil is used mainly in cooking. The plant needs full sun or brightness and a rich soil kept evenly moist. Don't fertilize the plant, or you'll affect the flavor. Pinch back leaves occasionally to encourage a bushy plant. The leaves have a spicy, almost cloverlike flavor that's an excellent complement to salads and egg, cheese, fish, and meat dishes. Use basil leaves fresh or dried.

84

Borage

An annual that grows to 24 inches, borage is a branching plant with pretty blue flowers and gray-green leaves that are covered with small hairs. Borage is somewhat hard to grow at home, but not impossible if you grow it in a somewhat lean soil—one that's only moderately wet, never soggy or dry. The leaves have a flavor like cucumber and add a distinctive taste to salads.

Chamomile

Chamomile is excellent when used as a tea. The plant grows only about 3 inches tall and has aromatic leaves. Chamomile needs a moist, well-drained soil and sunlight to prosper.

Chives

Chives are quite easy to grow at home. As soon as the plants are a few inches high, snip off the tops for cooking. Use the tops chopped in salads and egg dishes.

Marjoram

The annual marjoram (a perennial when grown outdoors) needs full sun and an evenly moist soil. Keep the plant trimmed and the flowers cut or it will get woody and leggy. Use marjoram fresh or dried in salads, meats, and casseroles.

Rosemary

Rosemary, a perennial, is rather large (some types reach 5 feet), so for indoor gardens grow the variety "Prostratus," which grows to only 24 inches high. Rosemary will thrive in almost any condition as long as the soil is well drained. Use the fresh leaves in chicken dishes, stews, and with vegetables.

Sage

Sage, which has gray-green leaves, likes full sun and a somewhat lean, well-drained soil. Overwatering can quickly kill sage, so be careful. Use the fresh or dried leaves with lamb or poultry.

Savory

There are two savory plants: one is an annual called summer savory *(Satureia hortensis),* and the other is winter savory *(Montana* spp.). Both types have narrow, aromatic leaves. Grow summer savory in a "humusy" soil in full sun; winter savory likes a sandy soil and bright light. Savory leaves are sort of peppery and can be used dried or fresh with meats, fish, and eggs, or in vinegars.

Tarragon

This perennial needs a well-drained, rather rich soil, kept uniformly moist. Use leaves dried or fresh in salads and fish and egg dishes.

Thyme

A perennial, thyme needs warmth and a well-drained soil. Water the plant, and then let it dry out thoroughly before watering again. Clip back occasionally to keep the plant within bounds. Use thyme leaves fresh or dried in salads or fish and poultry dishes.

CHAPTER 9

Harvest Fruits

Only in the last few years have tropical fruit tree plants become available for growing. Suppliers have responded to the demand with a great abundance of fruits for indoor growing. Quite logically, suppliers realize that there are more people living in apartments and small places than in homes with backyards. But will the fruits advertised "for indoor growing" really grow indoors in containers? The answer depends both on the plants themselves and you, because you must take care of the plants.

When the first seeds of such tropical fruits as papayas, mangoes, and bananas, among others, became available, I immediately sent for them. I was quite interested in seeing if I could have papayas bearing indoors, as they do outdoors in Florida, my childhood home. It turned out that 80 percent of the plants I sent for were successful; the 20 percent that were failures may have been my fault (although I doubt it). I subsequently found out that bananas just won't bear indoors, and peanuts, too, were a failure for me as a crop. I never got a shell from my planter box of peanuts. But I did get a few papayas and mangoes. Once the plants germinated, I treated them in much the same way that I cared for my three hundred houseplants.

Once the crucial germination stage was past and plants were transplanted to individual tubs of soil, they more or less grew on their own. Because the new additions were self-fertile (each produced without a companion plant), there was no worry about pollinating plants. When growing fruit indoors just remember that with fruits, as with any other indoor plants, it's a matter of time, patience, care, and love. As you read the following pages, prepare yourself for full flavor.

Avocados

The lush green meat of the avocado, formally known as *Persea americana,* has furnished many a table with salads, and its rather heavy rounded pit has furnished many households with a lush green plant. Part of the avocado popularity is due to the fact that the pit is easy to get started. There are several methods of approaching the birth of your avocado. Some people (I'm one) merely clean the pit and put it in a glass jar half full of water. You can also prop the pit on toothpicks. In a few weeks it's off and growing roots. I then plant them in soil.

To be more certain of germination, however, cut a thin section from the apex and the base and peel away the papery pit coating. Put the pit in the soil or water with its base downward—that is, the broadest part of the pit. If in soil, don't embed the pit too deeply; cover it with about $1/2$ inch.

Be sure the avocado has sufficient drainage; although it isn't choosy about soil, it is particular about stagnant water at the roots. The plant has a tendency to shoot straight upward, so once it is growing well, clip off the top to encourage side branching or it will get leggy and unattractive. Even so, you may have to stake the plant to maintain a handsome appearance.

Repot the avocado frequently (every six months); each time put it in a larger pot. Eventually you'll have a handsome tree that will outgrow the windowsill and be suitable for outdoor growing where climate permits.

Bananas

Small banana plants (genus *Musa*) are now being sold for growing indoors. I can't guarantee you fruit, but I can tell you that you'll have a fairly nice-looking plant if you grow a banana container plant. They need sandy soil and lots of water, but will grow quickly in spring and summer (the balance of the year they just sit there). Use a 12-inch tub.

I've grown many types of banana plants and have yet to have a harvest—but I never expected one, so it's okay. Perhaps you will fare better with your plant. Banana plants are tropical and need warmth and attention—perhaps that's the answer.

Cherimoyas

Generally called custard apples, cherimoyas taste like a combination of pineapple, peach, and banana, and make a good dessert. The plants themselves are handsome, with light green, velvety leaves. Cherimoyas grow to about 6 feet indoors.

Plant the seeds ¹/₄-inch deep in a suitable starter mix and put the container in a room at 78° Fahrenheit. When the seedlings are about 6 inches tall, transplant them into 10-inch pots and continue to grow them as you would a houseplant; a sunny place and copious watering (less moisture in winter) are recommended. Germination period is generally 4 to 5 weeks, and the plants bear fruit within 2 years. Cherimoyas are quick-growing plants, but once they reach the fruiting stage, growth subsides indoors.

Harvest the fruit when it turns from brownish green to yellowish green, and keep the fruit at room temperature for 1 week before eating it. The fruit has a somewhat better flavor when it's chilled.

Chinese Gooseberries

Don't let the name throw you; what you'll be looking for is the kiwi fruit. The true gooseberry *(Actinidia ainensis)* is native to China, but the fruit we find at local markets is from New Zealand. This lovely twiner, with its fuzzy leaves, is ideal for the windowsill. The fruit itself is the size of a small egg but is shaped like a gooseberry and is chartreuse in color. When sliced and sprinkled with lemon the fruit is somewhat puckery but good; it's not an all-time favorite but worth a try. Don't eat the seeds in the center; plant them. Pick out the small seeds from the center of the fruit and dry them on a blotter or newspaper.

Because the kiwi is subject to our old nemesis, damping-off, sow the seed in a coffee can or flat azalea pot and cover it slightly with vermiculite to protect the stem-to-ground part. It takes about 8 weeks to germinate. If you have trouble sprouting the kiwi pits the first time around, give them a cooling-off period in the refrigerator before the second attempt. To do this, mix the dry seed with some sphagnum moss in a Baggie and store at 45° Fahrenheit for about 40 days. (This process supposedly stimulates the natural cycle the kiwi goes through in nature.) Then replant the seed in containers (coffee cans or shallow pots are fine). In the latter process you'll have sprouts within 3 weeks; transplant them to 10-inch pots when they're a few inches high. If you use the first method, pray hard.

Citrons

I found this delightful fruit in Chinatown during the winter season. Citron, botanically known as *Citrus medica,* is, under ideal growing conditions, a dwarf tree of about 8 feet with a large (6- to 8-inch-long) ovoid fruit. The fruit, which is rough-textured and fragrant, is the citron peel used for fruit cakes. There is really no need to grow this one for its fruit, but the plant itself is rather pretty, with leafy green toothed leaves. Meticulously peel the citron and reserve the peel for future use. Wash away all pulp and plant the seed or pit in some sandy soil in a shallow container. Bury the seed about 1 inch deep in the soil and keep warm (72° Fahrenheit). The sprouts should start in about a month. When large enough, about 4 inches tall, put the seedlings into individual pots with soil that contains some calcium. The citron is an evergreen tree, so be sure to keep watering it through winter, although in these months temperatures can be somewhat cool (50° Fahrenheit).

Coconuts

If you have never tasted the white meat inside a fresh coconut, you are missing something. It is good. And if you have never grown a coconut palm in your kitchen, you are missing something equally good. It is a handsome plant that lends a tropical note to gray days.

The nut itself is a hard outer shell or hull. One end is rounded, the other narrow. It is from the round end that the young shoot emerges. With coconuts you need two, one to eat and one to plant, because the whole nut, hull and all, must be used, and this is rarely the way they appear in supermarkets, but you can find them sold as novelties at various airport boutiques, especially in Florida where I got mine.

You will need a large tub to start your coconut, and I used a half barrel with rather poor soil and sand base mix as a starter. Do not bury the coconut; all you will have is a buried coconut. Rather, prop it in the container so the fat end protrudes about 2 to 4 inches higher above the soil than the other end. Keep the starting medium very moist. When sprouting starts at the end (and you will see it) it is time to transplant to a big tub with rich soil, with the coconut again protruding from the soil. Be sure the tub has excellent drainage facilities. The coconut likes lots of water but not water that just sits there. It must drain freely.

It will take about a year before the actual fronds open and the plant looks like a palm. When the fronds develop, it is time to cover the decayed portion of the nut. Use a good rich potting soil. In time the plant will decorate your room with lovely green, but don't ever expect anything more, like fruit, for example. This is beyond the power of the amateur gardener, or the advanced one, for that matter.

Date Palms

Dates, botanically named *Phoenix dactylifera,* are infinitely good for you and loaded with all kinds of vitamins, and date palms are lovely indoor trees, so there are two reasons not to dismiss this venture with a shrug of the shoulders. Don't make the mistake of using pasteurized dates that have been steamed and preserved with chemicals. This is a mistake nutritionally speaking too. Get the pure dates, that haven't been tampered with, at health-food stores. After you have finished your date dessert, wash the pit or pits (it's best to start several), and put them in a starter mix. The time for germination varies, but it could be as long as 2 months, so don't give up in disgust. Keep the container in a warm place with good humidity (use the Baggie-on-a-stick method.)

The seed cotyledon that acts as a reservoir for food for most plants usually comes from the top or above ground—not so with the date. It comes from the bottom, and it travels throughout the soil (like a root), coming up many inches later. When the root is about an inch long above the soil, it is time to transplant to a large tub of rich soil so the plant can continue to grow (hopefully). In a few weeks the root or what was a root, or maybe is a root, will be joined by another, and presto, fronds! Your date is on the way. Give the plant plenty of sun, good moisture, and occasional feeding to keep it gracing your home. Unlike many plants mentioned in this book that remain medium and small, with the proper care the date palm can grow into a large plant—all from a little pit. Such miracles keep gardeners like me alive.

Figs

A fig tree in the bedroom isn't too bad an idea; the trees have large-lobed leaves and a nice branching habit. Plant fig seedlings in large (20-inch tubs) of rich soil. Feed plants well through the spring and summer, but not so much the rest of the year. Figs do better in a bright place than in direct sunlight, and they need even moisture all year long.

Indoor figs are rather fast-growing trees and reach 5 to 6 feet in height; prune them once a year to encourage branching.

The fig is an interesting plant that's becoming quite popular with indoor growers. Look for fruit on your plants in late summer; you won't have a bushel of figs, but you may have a harvest.

Litchi Nuts

You've eaten these, no doubt, in Chinese restaurants, where they're served either within a dish (succulent and sweet) or dried (sweet and dry). From southern China, the litchi, known in the plant world as *Litchi chinensis,* has been around for more than 2,000 years. For your purposes, you'll need fresh litchis; the dried ones won't grow. So go to Chinatown to get them. The smoother-skinned pit, dark brown-black in color, is pretty in itself without planting, but once planted it produces a lovely narrow-leaved plant. Litchi is difficult to get started, so sow several seeds, one to a 6-inch pot, in an acid-rich soil. Plant them about ¹/₂ inch deep. Keep litchis well watered and shaded, gradually exposing them to bright light but never direct sun. If you don't see signs of growth in 2 or 3 weeks, you've erred—it's probably a dried litchi fruit pit, which will do nothing.

Mangoes

The mango fruit is becoming popular because it's now available in many supermarkets; it's a delicious breakfast or dessert treat. The fruit is yellow and red with black specks, and is usually kidney-shaped. You can get small mango trees from southern suppliers, or you can simply start your own from a seed.

After you've eaten the fruit, scrub the bristly-haired pit with a brush; then let the pit dry for a few days. Set the pit on end with the eye up, and suspend it with toothpicks in a jar of water (similar to starting an avocado pit). Or start it in a sterile medium such as vermiculite. Insert the bottom inch or two of the pit into the medium. Put the container in a warm, bright place; in 4 to 6 weeks the seed should germinate. When the seedling is 6 inches high, transfer it to a 10-inch pot, keeping the soil evenly moist and the plant in sunlight.

Even if the mango doesn't set fruit for you—and it might not—it still makes an attractive indoor plant. Besides, who else can boast a mango in the bedroom?

Melons

Growing melons indoors seems unreasonable—and in most cases it is. However, there are now some midget varieties (Sugar Baby and others) that produce melons about the size of large grapefruits; conceivably they could bear indoors if you start them in large tubs in May or June in a hot, very sunny window. Melons require a great deal of water and high heat to do their best. The midget varieties are supposed to be more productive than their larger cousins, so you can have melons indoors.

Start seeds as described in chapter 2, and use huge (16-inch) wooden barrels or tubs. Plant only one plant to a tub, because melon plants grow rapidly and produce large lovely leaves. Since melons are vining plants, they'll need some support; a trellis inserted into the soil works well. Keep tying the vine to the wooden support so you'll have a vertical garden and not a mass of tangled stems.

Melons are for the adventurer who likes to accomplish the unusual. Picking a melon out of your bathroom is indeed an accomplishment—and it can be done.

Passion Fruits

Passion fruit, sometimes called purple granadilla, is excellent for desserts (with cream) or for jellies (the flavor is like strawberry), and is loaded with minerals. The attractive vining plant has large-lobe leaves.

Start passion fruits in the spring from purchased seeds. Sow the seeds $1/4$ inch deep in vermiculite or a similar starting medium. Keep sown seeds in bright light, at 78° Fahrenheit. When the seedlings are about 4 inches tall, transplant them into 10- or $1/2$-inch tubs.

Keep passion fruit plants in a bright, but not sunny, place. Give plants only moderately moist soil; it's better to underwater than to overwater. Add 2 tablespoons of lime to a standard houseplant soil, and give the plants scant moisture until they're at least 12 to 18 inches tall; thereafter, water routinely, but reduce moisture in winter. The plants bear in about 24 months.

Passion fruits are oval, have many seeds (surrounded by orange-colored pulp), and have a very aromatic fragrance. Harvest fruits when they reach the fragrant stage.

Peaches

The Bonanza peach, about 4 feet high, bears fruit indoors—and even the novice gardener can't kill it. Buy the tree at nurseries when it's in season.

The peach tree needs a large (20-inch) tub of rich soil. Give the plant plenty of sun and lots of water, except in winter, when it should be somewhat dry. Feed the plant at every second

93

watering. Summer your peach tree outdoors to guarantee good results. The plant bears small pink flowers.

Harvest the fruit when it's soft to the touch and has a pretty peach color. Listing recipes here is unnecessary, because we all know how to eat peaches—fresh off the tree, or in a cobbler, or peach ice cream, and so on.

Persimmons

If you've ever seen the lovely persimmon tree, known as *Diospyros kaki,* you'll want a potted plant for the kitchen windowsill. It has ovate green leaves, and its bright orange fruit is eaten fresh or cooked. Germination is erratic and may take from two to ten weeks, depending on how you handle the seed. For best results put the seed in some sphagnum moss after you've eaten the fruit and store the seed and moss in a closed bag in the refrigerator for ninety days. Then sow the seed in an 8-inch container and cover with a shallow layer of soil; give it warmth and bright light and keep your fingers crossed. If all this sounds like too much of a struggle, remember that few people can boast a persimmon tree on their windowsill, even without persimmons.

94

Pineapples

You can't find a better or more undemanding houseplant than the pineapple member of the bromeliad family. It can be started easily by slashing off the crown of the fruit (the part with the leaves) about one inch below the base of the leaves. Let it dry to prevent rotting of the stem after planting. Put the crown in a 8-inch pot of sandy loam and place container and all on top of the refrigerator. The pineapple needs good bottom heat to get it going. Give the pineapple good drainage and frequent light waterings rather than occasional thorough caterings. If you want to buy a plant, they're available in florist shops but don't get the miniature one; it's temperamental. Ask for the real one by name: *Ananas comosus.*

Pomegranates

Many people are probably familiar with the small pomegranate, *Punica granatum nana,* sold as a houseplant. But you can also grow the standard pomegranate, *P. granatum,* from seed. Introduced into England from Spain in the sixteenth century, this delicious fruit makes a handsome indoor plant.

The fleshy substance around the pomegranate seed is what is eaten; it is cooling and sweet to the taste. Once you have eaten the goodies, take the seed and allow it to dry a few days. Then germinate the seed in shallow pans of vermiculite covered with a plastic Baggie to assure good humidity. Mold may accumulate on the seed, but don't panic—this is a symbiotic relationship necessary to germination. In about two months (if you're lucky) the seeds will crack open and growth starts. Now transfer the seedlings to individual pots of rich soil—equal parts potting soil and humus. Cover the seed and the taproot with the soil, and in a few weeks leaves should appear. Give the plant warmth and sun; the soil should be evenly moist, never soggy, and the pomegranate dislikes high humidity.

You can also separate seed from pulp (the part we eat) by running the fruit through a sieve and rinsing away the fleshy part. That is, if you don't like eating pomegranates.

Although eating and starting the seed of this plant is very possible even for the novice, getting the plant to bloom is another story and would require several more pages. So be content with the lovely foliage: It is a delightful pot plant.

Rambutans

This fruit, native to Malaysia, is beginning to appear in specialty markets. It belongs to the same family as the litchi and is grown in the same way. The fruit eaten—and it is good—is the white fleshy aril surrounding the single seed. It is sweet and acid and can be eaten raw, or it may be stewed. The seed has to be started in high humidity and good warmth in a sandy soil mix kept evenly moist. When germination occurs (and this may take weeks) and green growth shows, transfer the plant to a tub with rich soil. Keep evenly moist and warm. The rambutan is a leafy branching plant that makes a fine, quite distinctive indoor accent. Although you might have to search for the fruit, it is worth the time. The botanical name for this plant is *Nephelium lappaceum.*

Strawberries

Can you grow strawberries indoors? You sure can! Find a sunny, warm spot—perhaps in a kitchen—and get a long planter box or strawberry jar; soon you'll be harvesting your own morning breakfast.

As previously mentioned, the variety that will do best indoors is *fraise de boys;* it's small, grows well, and bears fruit on and off throughout the warm months. Plants need rich soil, plenty of water, and some feeding. Grow plants in the sunniest spot in your kitchen or bathroom window.

Standard strawberries will do well indoors in strawberry jars; however, they require more space and attention than *fraise de boys.*

Yellow Guavas

Rarely do you find guavas in grocery stores, yet this tropical fruit is crammed with vitamin C. You can eat guavas fresh, use them as pie fillings, or make jellies and jams from them. The plant has pretty oval leaves and a semibranching habit; indoors it grows to about 4 feet.

Plant seeds ¼ inch deep in vermiculite or another suitable starting medium, and keep the seed container at 78° Fahrenheit. (Use heating cables at the bottom of the container to ensure stable temperatures.) Germination occurs in about 3 weeks. After germination, thin out plants and select the strongest; repot the strong plants in a sandy soil (a standard houseplant soil with 1 cup of sand added). Use a large (14- or 16-inch) tub for your guava.

During growth, guavas need large amounts of water and feeding every two weeks. Always keep plants in a sunny spot indoors. In winter, guava naturally rests a little, so don't try to force it to grow—give it less water and stop feeding.

White flowers will appear in the summer. The tree will bear fruit in about 2 years and then will live for 6 or 7 years longer. After a while the plant will grow too large to be kept indoors, so cut back periodically by pruning the branches at the ends or grow outdoors.

Guava must be fully ripe—soft to the touch and yellow—when it's picked.

CHAPTER 10

Insect and Disease Prevention

Insects and diseases may attack your vegetables even if you carefully raise your plants. However, there are ways to prevent or eradicate these problems, and they can be done quite successfully without the use of harmful chemicals. Using old-fashioned remedies and botanical repellents, and allowing birds, lizards, frogs, and toads in the garden will go a long way in getting rid of pesky insects. For diseases, the fungicides sold at nurseries are quite effective and safe for you and your vegetables.

INSECT VARIABLES

Keeping plants healthy is the main step in preventing insect damage. Weather is another factor: Insects proliferate in certain kinds of weather. For example, certain larvae need a constant temperature of 80° Fahrenheit over a period of 5 days before they can hatch. The third variable is cleanliness; larvae accumulate and hatch in junk, so get rid of dead weeds, and never let vegetables lie on the soil. Keep a vigilant eye out for bugs, know what you are looking for, and know your foes.

Enemy Insects

Aphids are green, black, pink, yellow, or red, with soft bodies. They eat the stems and leaves of beans, cucumbers, eggplants, peas, peppers, squash, and tomatoes. Bean leaf beetles are reddish with black spots. They attack beans, leaving circular holes in plants.

Cucumber beetles are spotted or striped. Besides cucumbers, they attack squash, eating the leaves. Cutworms are hairy moth caterpillars that thrive on beans, peppers, and tomatoes. Earwigs, long and hard-shelled with pinchers, devour lettuce. Wedge-shaped leafhoppers go after beans and lettuce. Blister beetles attack peppers. Whiteflies dine on tomatoes, and root maggots prefer radishes.

Mexican bean beetles are copper colored with many spots who eat the leaves of beans, almost skeletonizing them. The Colorado potato beetle loves eggplant as well as potatoes. Rust flies are white maggots that lurk at carrot roots; they eat the roots and crown of the plants. Brown and flat squash bugs wilt plants, causing them to yellow. Squash vine borers are invisible to the eye; they wilt squash. Tomato hookworms are green and eat the leaves of tomatoes. Thrips are tiny yellow or brown bugs that love onions, causing white blotches on leaves.

Lacebugs are gray to light brown in color and flat with lacy wings. They prefer eggplant, turning the leaves of the plant yellow and brown. Pea weevils are black, humpbacked, snouted beetles; they eat holes in peas and the pods. Snails and slugs, considered insects here for our purposes, eat the leaves and fruit of all vegetables.

Old-Fashioned Remedies

Through the years, certain tried-and-true gardening methods have persisted, and for good reason: They work. As a bonus, you do not have to use chemicals that could harm you, animals, or the soil. Handpicking insects off vegetables is a highly effective way to get rid of the bugs so long as you are not squeamish. (This method is superb for slugs and snails, or use any snail killer that does not contain metaldehyde.) Just remember to wear gloves and use tweezers if necessary for especially stubborn insects. Foot powder, oddly enough, is also effective. Shake the insects and/or larvae from the plants, and then sprinkle some foot powder on them.

A soap and water solution eliminates many insects, including aphids. Make a solution from a 1-pound bar of laundry soap and 2 gallons of water. (Be sure to use soap, not detergent.) Douse plants with the solution and then rinse them off with clear water. Sticky bands and collars that fit around containers or plants are quite good for controlling certain insects. These devices are sold at nurseries under various trade names.

A cardboard collar made from tar paper or sections of milk cartons stapled together will keep cutworms away. Lights are an excellent way to keep night-flying insects and cutworms away from the vegetables. Hang a lantern over a shallow pan of water and a float of kerosene. Commercially made electrical light traps are quite good but also expensive.

Botanical Repellents

Botanical repellents are made from plants and are generally safe. Pyrethrum, rotenone, quassia, ryania, and hellebore are all available commercially; just be sure to double check the label to ensure that the manufacturer has not combined the botanicals with persistent poisons.

Pyrethrum is derived from a species of chrysanthemum. The pulverized flowers are toxic to insects and kills aphids, whiteflies, and leafhoppers on contact.

Rotenone is from the derris root, a woody climber. The ground root effectively wards off aphids, cutworms, pea weevils, and houseflies.

Ryania is a shrub native to Latin America. The solution incapacitates squash bugs, cabbage loopers, and other insects. Quassia is a tree from South America. Its roots and bark are so intensely bitter that various insects will not come near the plant. Hellebore, from the lily family, has a burning, acrid taste.

You can grow several of these plants yourself and brew your own repellents if you are so inclined. Dry chrysanthemum flowers (*C. cinerariaefolium* or *C. roseum*) on sheets of newspaper in a well-ventilated spot; pulverize the dried flowers and mix the dust with water. Soak rotenone and hellebore roots overnight in a bit of water. Crush them the next day and boil them in water; the extract is the insecticide.

Vegetable Garden Friends

Birds, lizards, toads, and frogs are definite assets in your vegetable garden because they will eat many of the bad bugs. The blue-tailed skink, which is black with a bright yellow line down its back, feasts on many insects. The fence lizard is also a superb insect hunter and does not disturb the garden. Salamanders are about 6 inches long and have smooth shiny black or slate-colored skin with yellow spots. They usually feed at night, devouring grubs, snails, earthworms, some spiders, and sowbugs.

Much of a frog's diet consists of insects. Toads consume great quantities of insects at amazing speeds. They take in the prey with their long tongues. The American toad, common to eastern North America, is 3 to 5 inches long. The southern toad, also 3 to 5 inches long, is found in the southeastern United States. The western toad lives in the prairie states westward to California. Toads can eat four times the capacity of their stomach in a 24-hour period. Not often seen but a gem in the garden is the large toad, 9 inches long and native from southern Texas to South America, This toad eats army worms, beetles, moths, and other pests. If you can get toads to settle in, they will be with you always because they have a strong homing instinct.

PLANT DISEASES

Your best defense again fungus diseases is using disease resistant seeds and prestarts, sold at nurseries. But still, disease may strike, so know the symptoms. From the symptoms you can diagnose the disease and buy the appropriate fungicide at the nursery. (Be sure to read the label to know when to stop spraying before harvest; generally the time is 2 to 3 weeks.)

Bacterial blight makes water-soaked spots on bean leaves. On peppers, it causes brown to black spots on leaves in addition to water-soaked spots. When it attacks peas, it causes dark-colored streaks on stems and round dark spots on leaves.

Anthracnose attacks beans, cucumbers, and squash. It causes dark reddish areas on bean leaves and makes round reddish brown or black spots on the leaves of cucumbers and squash. Fusarium wilt likes peas, yellowing and stunting plants. Leaf blight turns carrot leaves yellow and then brown. Powdery mildew coats tomatoes with a grayish powder.

Bacterial wilt withers pea vines and stunts eggplant. Bacterial spot causes greasy spots and yellow margins on eggplant leaves.

CHAPTER 11

Specialties

This chapter offers a myriad of exotic vegetables for your eating enjoyment. These ethnic gems are enormously interesting plants to grow, and a knowledge of which plants these special vegetables are derived from will add to your appreciation and enjoyment of the wonderful world of foodstuffs. Whether your tastebuds prefer the Asiatic ginger, bok choy, or snow peas, or whether you lean more toward the hotter vegetables from our neighbors in Mexico, here you will find that special food for your eating pleasure.

GREENS

There is more to the world of greens than lettuce; escarole (endive), watercress, bibb lettuce, sorrel, and chicory are all wonderful gourmet greens that will add to your enjoyment of vegetables. Many of these specialties often cannot be found at the local supermarket, but growing them in containers ensures you of a ready supply and saves you money. As a bonus, these greens are easy to grow, even with minimum conditions.

Chicory

This perennial herb comes in many forms. The one most people are familiar with has very curly leaves and is used in salads.

The developing crown of chicory grown in darkness or semi-darkness and then blanched and used as a vegetable or in salads is known as endive. It has a fine and delicate (if somewhat bitter) taste that adds zing to salads or is fine by itself when cooked in a frying pan with a dash of onion added. The dried ground roasted root of chicory is used to flavor or adulterate coffee.

Radicchio, a form of chicory, is a very trendy vegetable that is especially popular in salads. It can be grown like any type of lettuce; it does well in tubs. Use friable soil and keep it well watered. Hanging baskets are also suitable containers for radicchio. If you hang the baskets in the kitchen, you can pluck radicchio leaves as they mature and use them in your cooking.

Escarole

Sometimes classified along with chicory in seed catalogs, escarole is actually quite different from chicory. It is a stalklike vegetable, crisp and bright green. Wash escarole carefully to remove all dirt; grow it as you would lettuce.

Sorrel

Sorrel is a perennial winter vegetable; it grows well in pots or tubs on the porch or patio. The average person does not hear much about this tasty treat, which has an arrowhead-shaped leaf and a tiny root. The root eventually splits, and plants then bear more leaves.

Sorrel is wonderful when added to salads, soups, and even omelets. (The green by itself can be made into a wonderful soup; consult a good cookbook for a suitable recipe.) I have successfully grown sorrel from seed in Napa, California, in a tub on my porch. This green prefers a sandy, well-drained soil kept moist.

Watercress

Watercress is by far more than just a dainty filling for tea time sandwiches; it is quite versatile and tasty. Sometimes called cress, it is part of the Crucifer family. The best known watercress in the United States is a variety of nasturtium known as *Roripa nasturtium*. This is a perennial herb that is not at all easy to cultivate, but with patience it can be grown in a container. Because it is so expensive when bought in stores, watercress is worth growing at home.

Give plants a very rich, almost mucky, soil. Running water must wash over plants, which is not an easy feat. Try flushing plants with running water daily. Watercress is superb in soups, salads, and various types of sandwiches.

ONIONS

Most of us think of onions as the white or yellow kinds in the produce section of the supermarket, but the onion group also includes the delicious shallots, chives, leeks, scallions, and garlic.

All these treats belong to the Allium group; many Alliums are prized as ornamental garden plants, and some are desirable as cut flowers because of their globular-shaped inflorescence. The food Alliums, however, all need different growing conditions, as we now discuss.

Chives

Chives are quite popular with vegetable lovers, who grow them in pots on windowsills. They keep growing even as you keep snipping off the pieces you need for cooking. Chives are wonderful additions to many dishes.

Grow plants from seeds or divisions. They are not fussy about sun or shade, but they do like water. Alternately place pots indoors and then outdoors, and you will have chives almost year-round.

Garlic

Besides tasting so good in so many dishes, garlic has proven to be very healthful and useful for averting various ailments. Garlic, like shallots, comes in the form of a bulb or corm; you separate and peel the bulb as you use it. Garlic bulbs are called cloves. Skins are white, pinkish, or rose. Grow cloves in pots of sandy soil and use the cloves as needed. The Burpee Seed Company offers many strains (varieties) for your cooking pleasure; consult their catalog for more information.

Leeks

Leeks are not easy to grow, they take up space, and they must be transplanted and fussed over. But they are so incredibly good in various dishes that they are worth the effort. Grow plants in tubs on the porch and deck, and be prepared to wait: Leeks take at least 4 to 8 months to mature. For example, seeds planted in June will produce sometime in March. Buy seeds from the catalogs of Burpee or Thompson & Morgan.

Wash leeks carefully to remove all sand and grit, which lodge between the handsome green leaves. Leeks are the key ingredient in the cold soup vichyssoise.

Scallions

Also called green onions, Welsh onions, or spring onions, scallions look like little onions with tails of clustered green tree leaves. The plants are part of the Allium family but sometimes are attributed to the Lily family. Besides being tasty in salads, scallions are great when eaten raw, with the bulbous end dipped into salt. But be warned: Scallions are very hot; some varieties can burn your tongue.

Grow scallions in sandy soil. Water the soil regularly, and keep containers in a somewhat sunny location.

Shallots

Shallots get my vote as the best onion to use in salad dressing and for frying with other vegetables. They are quite expensive in the store, but you can grow them inexpensively in a container indoors or outdoors.

Plant store-bought clumps in the fall, winter, or early spring in 6- to 8-inch pots filled with a loose and sandy soil that drains readily and is enriched with a dash of bonemeal. Break off the gray or brown clumps as needed (you can keep them in a dry location for weeks). Peel the clumps when you are ready to use the shallots in your recipes (and dozens of recipes call for shallots). You can also chop the small and hollow foliage and use it in salads. The plants multiply rapidly, so you can give some to friends.

Asian Vegetables

Chinese vegetables have always been popular, but they have become even more so since the increase of interest in wok (stir fry) cooking, the healthfulness of the vegetables themselves, and the wonderful taste of these foods. All Chinese vegetables adapt readily to container growing. And now some of the Japanese foods are gaining favor here, including daikon, a form of radish.

Ginger, long a staple in China, provides excellent flavoring to many different dishes, including some American recipes. Bean sprouts and bok choy enhance many forms of food; bok choy is a favorite in wok cooking. Taro root, snow peas, water chestnut, and lotus root are all aquatic vegetables that you can tackle as an adventure and that will add to your culinary skills.

What you grow and how you grow it depend on your personal preference. True, it is easier to buy rather than grow some vegetables, such as canned water chestnuts, but exotics such as taro root and lotus are hard to find in stores. Most Asian vegetables are worth growing, and they will thrive in tubs or large containers on the porch or the patio.

106

Bok Choy

Also called Chinese cabbage, bok choy is a crucifer that is easy to cultivate. It adapts well to many dishes and can be cooked in various ways, but its main use is as an ingredient in stir fry. Use both stalks and green parts. Grow seed in large tubs filled with well-draining soil.

Daikon

This radish is hard to find in markets, but it is easy to grow from seed (order seeds from a mail order supplier). Plants need a rich friable soil kept evenly moist. Usually, within 1 month to 6 weeks the radish is ready for use. It can be used raw as a garnish, but it can also be cooked (remove the root). Even the pretty vivid green foliage can be cooked and seasoned to taste, providing superb eating.

Ginger

Ginger root is available in most stores. Plant the roots, and when they sprout, keep dividing them as they grow on. The best-known ginger is *Zingiber officinale,* a plant I grew years ago as a foliage specimen without realizing how good the root is for cooking.

Plant the root sprout side up in a moist soil in an 8- or 10-inch pot with excellent drainage. Plants must have sun and even moisture; keep ginger at average home temperatures. Do not peel the ginger root to use it, simply slide a piece off and chop or grate it as needed. The taste is zesty and somewhat hot. Many tasty duck dishes call for the addition of ginger.

Snow Peas

Snow peas, at long last, are now being sold in many stores, but they are easy to grow at home. A variety of the common pea, snow peas do well when cultivated in a 10-inch pot filled with friable soil. Water the plant evenly, and be sure drainage is excellent. Place the container on a deck or porch in protected yet somewhat sunny location. Snow peas grow from seed without much care, and they make for incredible eating.

Taro Root and Lotus Root

These two vegetables are seldom seen in stores, but they are fun to grow in water at home. Taro is a bog plant, but it will grow in moist soil as well. The root is somewhat like a corm; the taro we are familiar with is *Colocasia escuelenta,* a foliage plant generally grown as a houseplant. It takes up some space, so grow it in large pots. Because it will not grow as a true aquatic plant in a container, keep the soil quite moist and place the container in a somewhat shaded location. The young shoots and the roots are edible. Taro root is the main ingredient of Hawaiian poi; check cookbooks for recipes.

The lotus root is called nelumbo and is used in various recipes. Lotus blossoms are prized for their beauty. Grow the plant (available at larger plant shops) in a sunken wooden tub or a sawed-off wine cask filled with a mucky soil. Rhizomes will multiply on their own if left alone and not subjected to freezing.

Water Chestnut

Actually fruits rather than vegetables, water chestnuts are difficult to grow, so, as previously mentioned, buy them canned. Water chestnuts are great when chopped and added to salads or sliced and stir fried.

MEXICAN VEGETABLES

The popularity of vegetables native to our neighbor from the south just keeps increasing, even though these taste treats are hard to find in non-Latino neighborhoods. Definitely worth growing in containers, Mexican vegetables offer incredible eating. I am especially fond of jicama, which is nice and crunchy in salads, and cactus pads (nopales), which add a nice seasoned tang to your eating repertoire. Other excellent Mexican vegetables include Mexican peppers (jalapeños), chayote, malanga, and calabaza—all will make what could be mundane meals veritable adventures in eating.

Cactus

Called nopales, these plants from Mexico and Guatemala are quite tasty, although they do require some patient preparation: I remember cutting out the tiny thorns from an Opuntia cactus pad to make a vegetable dish. Slice the pad into strips. Steam the strips and then season.

Nopales are easy to grow in a large tub on the deck or in the yard; the taste of the pads is quite different. Plants need a sandy soil that drains rapidly. If you can find the pads at a store, you will be shocked at how expensive they are. A friend of mine paid $2 for one pad! Consult a good Mexican cookbook for numerous recipes featuring nopales.

Chayote

From Mexico and Guatemala, chayote is a member of the squash family. It is also called custard marrow, merlitons, and vegetable pear. It has been used in other countries for quite a long time but is seldom seen in stores in the United States.

Chayote is a vine that produces brilliant green pear-shaped fruit throughout the year. It has a delicate flavor, similar to a cross between a zucchini and a radish. Chayote is usually steamed or boiled and seasoned and served as a vegetable. It can also be used in soup.

Grow chayote from seed in a large tub of well-drained soil kept evenly moist. This fast grower requires a sunny location and a trellis to grow on.

Jicama

Pronounced hee-kah-ma, this is a large woody vine from the morning glory family, widely grown in Mexico and occasionally in the United States. Jicama has showy white flowers and a tuberous root; it is the root that is used in cooking and sliced and diced in salads. It can also be used in soups. Available in specialty stores, jicama is expensive.

Malanga

Also called taro, this aroid is from the plant family Xanthosoma. Malanga is a root vegetable with tuberlike corms that are stem-shaped and about 12 inches long, 3 inches wide. Young leaves are excellent for using as pot herbs. The roots are covered with a tough brown skin that must be peeled away.

Boil the roots to make them tender; they are excellent in soups and salads. Grow the plant in a container that is not in direct sun. Do not overwater; treat malanga as you would if growing lettuce. This can be a difficult plant to raise, so be patient.

Peppers

There are peppers and there are peppers—hot, sweet, medium hot, and so on. The typical jalapeño pepper from the Southwest is about 1 inch across and 4 to 6 inches long. Although green in color, its taste is red hot. Plants grow well in small pots and take about 80 days to mature. Use them with caution.

Other peppers are also available to grow, such as the Thai pepper and the Hungarian wax pepper; the Thai pepper is orange at maturity, the Hungarian is yellow.

Tomatillo

You can sometimes find these in stores, but more often you will have to grow your own, and the tomatillo is wonderful in dishes such as chili relleños and enchiladas. This looks like a tiny tomato with a brown husk. The plants grow large—to about 5 feet—so if you want something different try growing the tomatillo.

Yucca

The yucca flower is great for cooking with pork. I am so fond of the petals that I often use them in my cooking. Blossom spikes bear hundreds of white-cupped flowers. Cut the stalks, then pluck the blossoms and wash them well. You can cut the flowers into salads, but they are even better pan-fried with pork and onions and wrapped in a corn tortilla.

Yucca is very easy to grow. Buy a small plant at a nursery and grow it in sun in well-watered rich soil. Blossoms appear in the summer; pluck stalks when plants are mature. I keep the blooms dried in a plastic package with air holes for several weeks. Yucca is hard to find in stores; growing it is the best way to have this delicacy.

CHAPTER 12

Community Gardening and Free Help

The most difficult part of community gardening is getting permission for use of the land or finding a source of land. But the effort is worth it because so many benefits are derived from a neighborhood garden: a sense of community spirit, fresh produce at little cost, an opportunity for children to indulge in gardening, and an improved appearance to the area selected. Publicizing your need for land and any efforts you are making in a local newspaper may help you obtain the necessary permission, or find out if a local school, gardening club, church, or private citizen has land you can use. Large companies that own land might contribute, and sometimes local politicians or county officials know of land that your group can use. Your local planning office may also help.

GETTING STARTED

Once you have the land and any necessary permission, you need a leader, someone who will organize the drive for workers and coordinate materials and time—someone who will get it all together. Next, divide the land into equal plots for each group of people, or let all the people share the entire amount of land. It should be noted, however, that people seem happier with their own little area rather than sharing an entire plot.

Now the land has to be cleaned and made ready for boxes and containers. Plant seeds or prestarts as we discussed in chapter 2. Keep seeds or seedlings evenly watered. This demands constant watering for the first few weeks. You need an around-the-clock watering scheduling the first 2 weeks, so appoint people to do the watering on certain days.

COMMUNITY GARDENS

After you secure permission from planning authorities, private citizens, church groups, or other sources to use the land for a garden, select one person to spearhead the drive and coordinate materials and time. You will need someone willing to devote some time to getting it all together. Once the land and leader are selected, divide the land into equal plots, with one plot to each family or group, or the entire garden can be shared by a group of people. It is far better for each family to have its own garden than for many people to try to cultivate a large area together.

The first step is to clean the land of debris by the hand-and-rake method—hard work but worth it. Next, have the land turned over. Rototilling is the easiest and best method; rototilling gets the land ready fast for growing and saves time and muscle work. (See the yellow pages for earth-moving companies.)

When the land is tilled, order some good topsoil. This is expensive, but if you want a good yield of vegetables, you will need fresh, nutritional topsoil. A 6-yard truckload of topsoil generally costs about $65, and for the average 25 x 100 plot, two truckloads can do the job. Spade and mix the topsoil into the ground and break up all soil so you have a bed that is porous and well turned.

Planting the garden will be little problem; it is fun to get the seeds or prestarted plants in the ground, so everyone will be willing to participate. Sow seed as described in the vegetable chapters (chapters 5 and 6), and refer to those chapters for when and how to plant. Once seeds are in the ground (and remember to leave ample space between rows for walking and tending plants), you must be sure that the seeds or seedlings get even moisture. This is the hard part because for the first few weeks constant watering is almost essential to get things growing. Select members of the group to water on specific days, say, one person for Monday and Wednesday, another person to do it Friday and Sunday. In other words, keep an almost round-the-clock schedule for watering the first 2 weeks.

KEEPING IT GROWING

Start picking weeds the minute you see them so they do not sap the soil of nutrients that the vegetables need. I do not believe in weed killers, so I suggest you hand pick. If this is done twice a week, hand picking is not that gruesome and provides good exercise. Again, select certain people to weed and thin on designated days, and have all phone numbers posted on a call sheet in case someone gets sick or cannot tend to the garden on a particular day. Then he or she can call and get a substitute.

Thin, weed, and water plants through harvest time, and once a week have everyone assemble to see how things are going and growing. The more team spirit, the better the garden. And once the first radishes and carrots are harvested, there will be little problem in finding participants to help in the next garden planting.

113

Harvest the vegetables when they are ready, dividing the harvest as equally as possible so everyone gets their full share (do not forget the kids get into the act too).

In my zest to get you started in community gardening I have neglected to mention the insect-prevention details. Have a knowledgeable person, one who has had some experience in gardening, protect the community garden plants against insects and diseases. This individual must be one who realizes the full importance of keeping the land clean of pests; without proper control, the entire garden could be wiped out. (Refer to chapter 10 for full details on how to cope with the insects.)

WHERE TO LOOK FOR FREE LAND

Here are some suggestions for getting the land for these gardens:

1. Look to *schools,* which may contribute some land to the program.
2. Ask *large companies* with land holdings if they would contribute some land (they might, for good public relations).
3. Seek out *church groups;* many churches own vacant land.
4. Run small inexpensive *ads* in *local papers* asking for privately owned land for use for vegetable growing.
5. Ask local *politicians/county officials;* they may have access to land areas that can be used for family farming.
6. Consult your *local planning office* and ask for land for vegetable growing.
7. Get your project known by newspapers or any other *media.*

SHARING THE BOUNTY

The idea of urban gardening and farming on empty city land is gaining momentum, and rightly so. It offers many pluses: (1) improves the appearance of a neighborhood by utilizing land that may have become litter-strewn; (2) gives people a sense of community spirit and group effort (badly needed these days); (3) offers children a chance to participate in gardening; and (4) provides fresh vegetables at little cost.

114

How to get the soil ready, the seed growing, and the plants in the ground are of little concern. There is not too much cost involved; work is necessary, but once people know about the garden, they will participate for part of the bounty. And a local newspaper ad will be good publicity for the community garden. What is not usually so easy is securing permission to use open land for vegetable gardens; getting permission involves reaching the right people. But newspapers will help make your plea known, and your local city representatives and city hall can be contacted to get things started.

Some companies in large cities may provide garden space for their employees—an empty lot nearby or perhaps even the rooftop area. You may want to initiate such a program at your company; today, so many people are interested in gardening that you are bound to have enough people to participate in the program.

Also check with local botanical gardens; many times they have a gardening program for children and have already acquired a plot of land that can be used in community gardening.

Maintaining the Garden

Watch for weeds, which drain nutrients that the vegetables need. Pick weeds as soon as they are spotted. Handpicking is much safer than weed killers as well as being good exercise. Appoint certain people to do the weeding on certain days; everyone should have everyone else's phone number so they can get a substitute if they become ill. It is also quite important to watch for insects. One person, knowledgeable in insect prevention, should be in charge of this aspect of vegetable gardening. Without proper insect control, the entire community garden may be lost.

Continue weeding, thinning, and watering plants until harvest time. During this maintenance, have weekly meetings so everyone can see how things are going, discuss what to grow, share methods of growing, and so on. In other words, do everything possible to encourage team spirit and keep it going. Be sure to let the children get involved in the harvesting.

115

Sources of Free Help

Your tax money does pay off in regards to gardening. Various government agencies can help you take care of plants. Agencies of the United States Department of Agriculture (USDA) Agricultural Extension Services, the United States Forestry Service, and various government publications are all available to help you with advice.

Government Services

To take advantage of free government services, you have to drop in at one of their offices, phone, or write. Personnel will give you advice at the office or over the phone; writing will get you informative pamphlets relating to your queries.

It is best to start at the local county level. The phone book lists all local, state, and federal agencies. If the people you call cannot help you, they will be able to tell you who can. When you call be prepared: Have definite questions and do not bother the personnel with vague or too-general questions. For example, if you have specific insect problems, call the county agent and explain the problem clearly.

The federal government is the largest source of published gardening information available. The USDA supplies pamphlets, booklets, and hardcover books dealing with plant diseases, seed growing, insect protection, and so on. Write the U.S. Department of Agriculture, Superintendent of Documents, U.S. Government Printing Office, Washington, DC 20250 for a list of their publications. Or you may call (202) 512-1800.

Large cities such as New York, Chicago, and San Francisco have central offices that carry the federal government publications you seek. Check local phone books for locations.

Another source of garden information is the Public Documents Distribution Center, Pueblo, CO 81009 for the list of selected U.S. government publications.

116

Suppliers (Mail Order)

There are many mail order suppliers; this list is partial. Other companies can be found in garden magazines advertisements. The mention of a company here is neither an endorsement nor a suggestion that one company has better products than another company. Catalogs are generally available, free or for a slight charge.

Burgess Seed & Plant Company
904 Four Seasons Road
Bloomington, IL 61701

Henry Fields Gardens
1 Meadow Road
Shenandoah, IA 51601

Gurney Seed & Nursery Company
Yankton, SD 57079

Herbst Bros. Seedsmen Inc.
1000 North Main Street
Brewster, NY 10509

International Growers Exchange
16785 Harrison
Livonia, MI 48154

Inter-State Nurseries
Hamburg, IA 51644

Earl May Seed & Nursery Company
Shenandoah, IA 51603

*Nichols Garden Nursery
1190 North Pacific Highway
Albany, OR 97321

Stern Nurseries
Geneva, NY 14456

*Sheperd's Garden Seeds
7839 West Zayante Road
Felton, CA 95018

R H Shumways
P.O. Box 1
Graniteville, SC 29829

Stokes Seed Company
Stokes Building
Buffalo, NY 14240

Thompson and Morgan
Jackson, NJ 08527

*Specialty and Ethnic Vegetables

Beneficial Insects Suppliers

The following insectaries provide natural enemies of insect pests:

American Biological Supply Company
1330 Dillon Heights Avenue
P.O. Box 3149
Baltimore, MD 21228

Beneficial Insectary
14751 Oak Run Road
Oak Run, CA 96069

BioLogic
P.O. Box 177, Springtown Road
Willow Hill, PA 17271

Nature's Control
P.O. Box 35
Medford, OR 97501

Index